INDIA'S DEVELOPMENT PARADIGMS

INDIA'S DEVELOPMENT PARADIGMS

S.N. Singh
K. Kishore

ANMOL PUBLICATIONS PVT. LTD.
NEW DELHI - 110 002 (INDIA)

ANMOL PUBLICATIONS PVT. LTD.
H.O.: 4374/4B, Ansari Road, Daryaganj,
New Delhi-110 002 (India)
Ph.: 23278000, 23261597
B.O.: No. 1015, Ist Main Road, BSK IIIrd Stage
IIIrd Phase, IIIrd Block,
Bangalore - 560 085 (India)
Visit us at: www.anmolpublications.com

India's Development Paradigms

First Edition, 2009

ISBN 978-81-261-4042-8

PRINTED IN INDIA

Printed at Balaji Offset Press, Delhi.

Contents

PREFACE

The theme of development has attracted global attention of scholars. Some of us at times express that a debate on development is a fashion, whereas for others it may be a serious concern, a concern in search of answers to the problem facing countries, particularly the third world in terms of poverty, hunger, unemployment, illiteracy and the like which are continuously affecting the quality of life, specially the poor. Increasing gap between the rich and the poor despite efforts, has been a cause of serious concern for the policy planners. The problem of regional imbalance alongwith socio-economic disparities has been persisting for decades is still evading an adequate explanation. Owing to these and similar other problems, there is a question mark on the strategies and models of development adopted during all these decades in India.

Subsequently, the decade of nineties witnessed a change in terms of new-economic policy which provided for liberalisation, privatisation and globalisation. This paradigm shift was expected to provide a new thrust to the economy by opening it to the world and encourage competition. The corporate sector was going to get primacy in the governing process with a new thrust. It is more than a decade since these reforms were introduced in the country. A logical question is thus, posed. The question posed is about the impact of these reforms on socio-economic scenario at the macro and the micro levels. Whether the paradigm shift has reduced State intervention in the development process? Whether the paradigm shift has helped reduce poverty and increase employment? There have been several such posers which asked for an objective assessment. This study has taken about three years to make an objective and rational assessment of the issues referred to. The present book is the final outcome of our effort in order to get a wider attention and circulation.

ACKNOWLEDGEMENT

Any effort of this nature needs the support and cooperation of various organisations and individuals in order to succeed. We, therefore, are duty bound to express our thankfulness to such organisations and individuals whose support and cooperation we received during the course of study. First of all, we express our thanks to the University Grants Commission, New Delhi, for their support without which it would not have been possible to undertaken this task. We are thankful to the officials and non-officials of the concerned States and the districts respectively for providing the necessary data and information. We thank the research staff, particularly Dr. K.K. Srivastava and Dr. S.S. Chauhan for providing the necessary help in collection of data. We are thankful to our colleagues in the Department, Dr. Manoj Dixit, Dr. Nand Lal Bharti and Dr. Vaishali Saxena (Gupta) for giving valuable advice and comments from time to time. We are thankful to Mr. Y.P. Singh and Mr. U.S. Srivastava for extending the library support and Mr. K.B. Singh for the secretarial assistance. Our thanks are due to Mr. Pramod Kumar for getting the manuscript computer typed. In the end we express our indebtedness to our family members and friends who have stood with us all through.

S.N. Singh

K. Kishore

Chapter 1

Introduction

There remains a continuous research for a better life ever since the civilisations organised themselves. The emergence of the state is a testimony to these efforts and we see this in the Aristotelian dictum that 'state came into existence for life but continues to exist for good life'. Civilisations have grown and perished during this long journey of human existence. Modern world too, is faced with the challenge of such development, a development that can ensure sustained survival of man and his environment. Several theories and models have emerged for the growth and development which, at times resulted in the very negation of the same. There is a serious concern particularly in the third world countries where prosperity of some coexist with the poverty of plenty. There is a need to address these issues persistently. Our effort in the present context, is to look at development in the context of India with this perspective in view. It encompasses the role of the state in the development process and consequently see if the paradigm shift has any relevance so far as the poverty of plenty is concerned. However, before taking up these issues in the subsequent chapters, it is proposed to preface the discussion by defining the concept of development to facilitate the debate.

There are already considerable literature on the concept of development which also leads to confusion in the debate. It may, therefore, be pertinent to clarify the concept of development before attempting to explain its various facets. Interestingly, the word 'development' has generated a serious debate in contemporary world, both in the developed as well as the developing. The concept of development however, eludes any simple or single acceptable definition. One line of argument explains that the concept is fundamentally biological. While a concept of development may be used in respect to physical systems, and while it may refer also to systems of ideas, the term has been most commonly associated with the organisation of living structures and life processes.[1] The varied uses of the concept have in the main been based on descriptive and inductive approach. But the tremendous gain in modern physics and the dissolving of the matter itself in the face of such gains, has suggested for all sciences an approach different from yesterday's descriptive experience.[2] The philosophies of sciences, in particular, look to this hypothetico- inductive method as an effective way to establish the unity of sciences including the study of behaviour. But many accept this approach with reservation. Many empirical scientists also interested in bridging the gap between the living and non-living, expect to do so by manipulating materials in the laboratory rather than symbols. Various compromises have been offered to attempt to bridge this gap.[3]

Students of animal and human growth and behaviour who attempt to fit the developmental phenomena observe systematic relationships with other data, have frequently had recourse, in one manner or another, to the "level of organisations" doctrine. Granted that science or knowledge may have a basic unity, it is easier, for the moment, to view experimental embryology as constituting one level of phenomenon, the behaviour of rat in a maze as another, the juvenile delinquent in the stolen car as another, and the emergence of mercantile capitalism as still another. Each of these orders of phenomenon can be described and some rule of generalisation formulated that will predict (within a margin of error) the course of an individual member of the order will likely to follow over time.[4]

Not only do the biologist and the students of behaviour development have difficulty fitting phenomenon of growth or development into physical concepts, but they have a fundamental difficulty with the symbolic system into which their concepts and constructs must be cast.[5] Another kind of scientific explanation consists in presenting the actual conditions and factors under which phenomenon will occur together with scientific law which are illustrated by the productive interaction of the conditions and factors. This is the view many biologically oriented students of development hold today.[6]

The empirical scientists frequently distrust the deductive approach. This theory grows out of an intimate knowledge of observed data. Scientists occupied in their laboratories are usually too busy to make more than occasional ventures into the philosophy of science. Thus they defer to their latter, more reflective years.[7] Certainly the empirical approach in science is still vigorous. It has been described that "the best view of a mountain range is usually obtained from a distance, at close quarters, minor peaks, and even hills obstruct the vista of the whole range. To understand man and his universe is the goal of the scientific movement. These goals must always be kept in view, in order that we do not make mistake means for ends.[8]

If a unity of science is to be achieved, embraced in one general theory or system, the facts of biological development of the living system organising its structure and behaviour over the time towards greater complexity, and maintaining a unity of 'wholeness' with some stability must ultimately be accounted for.[9]

The concept of development usually has reference to ontogeny. Representatives of discipline which deal with individual organism present their understanding of the term and asses its usefulness in their several field. In the field of psychology the developmental point of view has been commanding increased attention with the publication of several recent works. The concept of development is sometimes used in reference to products or the human mind, representative for history and literature have their own ideas.

The word development is notoriously one with protean meaning. It is sometimes used to connote process, sometimes the product of a process. It is frequently employed as purely descriptive term to characterize several types of changes; but it also functions in many contexts as a emlogistic label.[10] In many of its current uses the world carries the suggestion that the developmental process may progressively manifest something latent or hidden. We speak of the development of heat in a wire of the development of a photographic plate, of the development of a fertilised egg, or of the development of a human personality, understanding in each case a sequence of continuous changes eventuating in some outcomes, however, vaguely specified, which somehow potently present in the earlier stage of the process.[11]

There are thus, several concepts of development which people have tried to visualize ranging from pure sciences like physics to social sciences. Our purpose is more akin to socio-economic parameters which have a different concept of development. We shall briefly analyze the same.

The concept of development incorporates different discussions reflected through different indicators. An important indicator of development is per capita income, which is determined both by the volume of production. It is basically a reflection of the level of productivity of an economy. Some of the other indicators of development are longevity of life and mortality and fertility rates. Apart from this core indicator, there are other indicators which contribute to the realisation of the central indicators, such as the productivity of the various production activities and education, condition of housing and roads and communication. Such factors jointly contribute to patterns of living, measured to fall at different levels of develcpment.[12] This indicates the phenomenon that higher the level of the indicator, higher is the level of development. Looking from another angle, development may be conceived in two ways: (i) as a unilateral course of change from what is enveloped i.e. unfolding what is latent into manifestation and (ii) as an instrument for the removal of binary possibilities of undergrowth and overgrowth. The two ways operate concurrently with respect to society, as more and equal, but differences in content according to two perspectives.[13] This gives us a different perspective of development.

Some also argue that development continues to be a matter of concern both at the conceptual as well as the operational levels. Attempts to evolve a comprehensive and convincing definition of development have failed mainly due to persistent inadequacy of comprehension about its ever – expanding role and subtleties of related specialisation at march of multidisciplinary intricacies in the midst of changing political and systemic realities.[14] Development is a widely participatory process of directed change in a society, intended to bring about social, economic, political and cultural development for the people through greater control over their environment.[15] This explanation suggests another perspective of development than we have attempted earlier.

Todays development debate has taken several sharp turns, indicating radical departures from five-decades. Old development theories, most of which talked of economic development as the central focus of all development endeavors. Now, when the economic model has caused greater disillusionment, the focus of the debate has shifted to social, cultural, political, technological and environmental aspects of development, each with its own rationale and recipies.[16] The critique of modern development theory are not restricted to alternatives, but are based on normative research for a more satisfactory and indigenous form of development, much different from dominant western paradigm (Kothari, 1988, 107.) Gunnar Myrdal offered perhaps one of the earliest and most stringent critique of the economistic bias in the western model of development couched in capitalists rationality. By the late sixties and early seventies the optimism of the western view of development began to fade in the light of the experience gained in the developing countries. One thing became very clear the development theories based on the western model of economic growth were found profoundly inadequate, and as such, were subjected to fundamental questioning.[17] In the ultimate analysis western model of development proved to be inadequate.

In the immediate post-war era, it was assumed that economic development was a historical process takes place in almost all societies, characterised by economic growth, Constitution of infrastructure, expansion of industry and increased protection and consumption of goods and services. Such was the assumption of the UN 1951 Study Measures for the Economic Development of Under-developed countries.[18] Over the half-century of development strategies since then, numerous approaches have challenged the assumption that development is a matter of almost exclusively of economic growth and increase in gross national product. Out of the inadequacies and also as a result of critique of scholars and practitioners and demonstration by civil society, the main bilateral and multilateral players in economic development have shifted to more holistic, equality and poverty based strategies that have more natural but with concepts of the right to development that did early growth oriented strategies.[19] This thus, added a new dimension in defining the concept of development.

By the end of 1980, the concept of 'Sustainable Development' had been launched by the Brundtland Commission which defines it as "development that meets the needs of the present without compromising the ability of future generation to meet their own needs" and gave overriding priority to the essential needs of the world's poor while acknowledging the same on the environments' ability to meet present and future needs. This approach has been endorsed by the entire UN System in the Rio and Johensburg Earth Summits and has had programmatic impacts, especially in the World Bank and the Organisation for Economic Cooperation and Development (OECD).[20] Drawing on the insight of Amartya Sen and the vision of Mahbub-ul-Haq, UNDP launched the idea of 'human development', which embraces human needs and social goals beyond national well being, such as higher standards of education and health, wider opportunities for work and leisure, increased capabilities and choices for the individuals.

Another dimension of development concept may be worth noticing here. The Comprehensive Development Framework (CDF) was introduced by the World Bank in October 1998 and launched in 1999. Its aim is 'achieving greater effectiveness in reducing poverty' by applying 'holistic approach to development' and reorganising the interdependence of all elements of development social, structural, human, governance, environmental, macro-economic and financial. Poverty reduction strategies were launched by the World Bank and the IMF and were the main focus of the CDF.

After having discussed several concepts and perspectives of development, a brief discussion of models of development in post-independent India is worth discussion here.

THE MODELS OF DEVELOPMENT ADOPTED IN POST-INDEPENDENT INDIA

Before discussing various models of development in post-independent India, it may be pragmatic to preface it by a review of the scenario at that point of time. It could well be seen that the nation was virtually shocked at the time of independence owing to partition which caused tremendous loss of human life and property on either side of the border. The immediate task before the top national leadership then was to first recover from the shock at the earliest and then estabilise the political system for future governance. A Constituent Assembly was constituted to provide for a Constitution for modern India which it did and this Constitution we gave to ourselves on November 26, 1949.

The basic tenets of governance have been enshrined in the Preamble of the Constitution.[21] The principles adopted were to determine the course of policy frames and governance for future India. However, for the purposes of development there is no specific provision. Consequently, we find that models and strategies developed and adopted during all these years were the product of individual genius of contemporary India. We would now try to look into various models and strategies adopted for growth and development in post-independent India.

At the dawn of independence the country was faced with the problems of shortage of food grains, lack of infrastructure in various sectors, social and economic inequality, poverty, to name only few. The immediate task before the government then was to make a policy choice for future development of India. The choice of planned development was deliberately provided by the government then headed by Pt. Jawaharhar Lal Nehru, who was impressed by the Soviet experiment of planning and development. Consequently India opted for a planned development approach for future development. A separate body in the name of Planning Commission of India, headed by the Prime Minister was thus constituted. The story of Five-Year Plans thus follows from here. A discussion about development under various Five-Year Plans has been taken up at appropriate places in the book.

One of the earlier models which India opted for its growth and development is known as Mahalanobis Model. Mahalanobis model assumed that development would trickle down from top to bottom. The advocates of this model also address this concept as 'trickle down theory'. This model laid emphasis on the development of heavy industries. This growth model postulated the technical relations between output, investment and labours in a four sector economy. Investment in heavy industries was designed to achieve industrialisation which was assumed to be the basic conditions for rapid economic development.

The stress on industrialisation which was not there in the First Five-Year Plan, became quite pronounced in the Second Five-Year Plan.

The impact of the adoption of this model used will be seen in India in the decade of 50s and 60s. Large scale investment in sectors like steel, power, fertilizers, irrigation etc. gave birth to many gigantic public sector industries in those days. Projects like Bokaro, Rourkela, Bhakra Nangal and the like were the visible testimony to this model. Impressed by these, Pt. Nehru once remarked that they are the 'temples of modern India'. It can, therefore, be argued that development of future India was seen through these big public sector undertakings, they were intended to provide the necessary infrastructure, a sound foundation for rapid economic development of future India. It was hoped that the 'trickle-down' effects of the growth of Gross National Product (GNP) could be able to address itself to alleviate poverty in the country.

With regard to the development of rural areas in the country a programme called Community Development Programme was initiated in the year 1952 itself. Community Development Programme can be considered a model of rural development in the sense it provided for a different approach for development in these areas with focus on community participation. It was advocated for the first time after independence that for proper development of the rural areas community participation is essential. Unless and until the community effectively participates in the development process, development will be difficult to achieve. Therefore, community development programme considered community participation the core for the development of the rural areas. However, the programme could not succeed as it failed to enlist community participation even though a new infrastructure was designed for the purpose.

The Government of India then appointed a Committee under the Chairmanship of the Mr. Balwant Rai Mehta in the year 1957 to look into the causes of the failure of Community Development programme and suggest measures for ensuring people's participation in the Development of the rural areas. The Committee examined the shortcomings in the erstwhile Community Development programme and the causes for its failure. Balwant Rai Mehta Committee thereafter, recommended for a new system to ensure the participation of the people in the process of development and decision making at the grass-root level. The model suggested by Balwant Rai Mehta came to be popularly known as *Panchayati Raj* – a three tier structure for governance in the rural sector. In order to ensure the participation of the people, the committee suggested an 'organic linking' of the three tier in the District, the Block and the Village through their peoples' representatives. It recommended for a direct election at lowest level i.e. the village. The rest of the tiers to be linked indirectly. Thus, Balwant Rai Mehta recommended for a P R model for rural areas i.e. the district and below for participative governance to ensure proper development of these areas.

The next two decades that followed witnessed the emergence of a *Panchayati Raj* system across the country with varying success in different States. But the model continued to be there in almost all the States of the Union. Subsequently we find change in later decades particularly in the 90's after the 73rd Constitutional Amendment Act was passed in 1992 which most of the States have accepted with changes as per their local needs and requirement. *Panchayati Raj* therefore, continues to be one of the models for rural India.

It may be noticed here that different experiments and models were being tried for the growth and development in the country but inspite of these efforts problems like poverty, unemployment, etc. in the rural areas were persisting. A new scheme in the name of Integrated Rural Development (IRDP) was launched by the Government of India during the Sixth Plan period as a sequel to Mrs. Gandhi's 'Garibi Hatao' slogan during the 1977 Lok Sabha election. The programme was launched as a direct attack on poverty. In this programme the Government instead of making use of the *Panchayati Raj* structure, it created another institution at the district level by the name of District Rural Development Agency (DRDA) with little elected element. This we can consider another model tried for the development of the rural areas in the country.

Apart from these a number of other programmes were launched by the Government of India to generate employment in the rural areas and try to improve the quality of life people living in the rural areas. However, inspite of these efforts little improvement could be seen so far as the poverty scenario in the rural areas was concerned. The gap between the rich and the poor continued to increase and there was little to show that the gap was bridging. Several research studies conducted in the country by various groups only strengthened these observations. There was therefore, serious concern at the highest level of the Government to re-address these issues.

THE ISSUES INVOLVED

India has been through more than five decades of planned development. During this long journey of planned development there are several issues which need an objective assessment. We have already noted in the earlier pages that the path of development in India has been an uneven one. Whereas certain sectors have registered growth while others have remained less fortunate. It raises a question mark on the strategies and models of development adopted during all these years. The question mark is because we find the problems that were there at the initial years of planned development phase, they continue to persist in one form or the other. It raises the issue for a renewed thought process.

The decade of nineties and thereafter, there is another effort through new economic policy. It marks a clear-cut shift in the earlier development policy. It marks a beginning for globalisation, liberalisation and privatisation. It opens up the nation's economy to the world market. The problem that we have been facing all these years was that of poverty, unemployment, illiteracy, etc. The issue therefore, to be addressed is how far this economic policy of liberalisation is going to help us in addressing our long standing problems referred earlier. Whether reduced State intervention in the development is going to help solve these problems or it is going to increase the burden on the poor. These are, therefore, issues which have to be addressed and a debate is still on.

THE DEVELOPMENT DEBATE

Owing to the continuance and persistence of the problems in the development sector which failed to resolve the issues like poverty, unemployment, inequitable distribution or whatever the fruits of development, questions have been raised about the very concepts and the perspectives of development. It has generated a serious debate across the world about the very purpose and notion of development. We would briefly try to put up the development debate in our own context.

As we have said earlier, India opted for a planned approach to development and a greater state intervention in the process of development to ensure equitable growth and justice. The initial decades of planned development in India presented the growth model. But this model could not deliver and failed to an extent to provide growth with justice. There is an emerging concern that we have gone wrong somewhere along the line and there is need for fundamental reconsideration for our development strategy. Such a realisation is rooted in the fact that in spite of the moderate rate economic growth in the country, a very large segment of our population still lives in utter poverty.[22] The increased GNP benefited the top echelons whereas the rest of the population remained largely unaffected. The development path that was pursued for long basically remained wedded to economic growth, favouring the strong, and depriving the weak.[23] The continued deprivation for long years has raised doubt amongst the concerned circles about the strategy adopted for development and therefore, a search for a new strategy which could address these issues afresh. It is a positive indication for a development debate in the contemporary scenario. The economic reforms encompassing liberalisation, globalisation and privatisation during the post-90's were aimed at a paradigm shift in the development process as well as development goals. The development process had witnessed considerable state intervention in the earlier decades. The new economic policy aimed at reduced role for the state in the development. The dependence of the people on the Government initiative was to be reduced deliberately. It was contemplated that by opening the economy to the world there will be increased competition which would gear up the economy. This would ultimately help the large section of the population to participate in the development process. Though it was mainly concerned with the corporate world, the rest of the society was supposed to get the benefit once he economy shows the upward trend. The next question is how far the poorer section of the society are going to benefit from this paradigm shift? Whether a lesser state intervention is going to help the poorer section of the society? There is, therefore, an issue for the debate to analyze the pros and cons of the paradigm shift in the development during the post-90 period.

In this debate following issues could be addressed-

i) The drawback of the earlier models of development the strategies adopted for the development.
ii) The main focus of the new economic policy.
iii) The extent of state intervention in the development process in various phase of development.
iv) The effect of paradigm shift on the general masses of people particularly the poorer sections of the society.
v) Major policy changes and their input on the development particularly the poorer section.
vi) To suggest measure for policy changes in case the new economic policy has failed to address the problem faced by the poorer section of the society.

NEED FOR THE STUDY

It is argued that more than a decade has passed since the economic reforms were introduced in the country. How far these reforms have helped the economy and the society grow, is a question of opinion. A development debate has been on in the country to focus on the various issues involved in the development process. Some argue that the economy has reached the take off stage and 8 to 10 per cent growth rate is in the offing. On the contrary, we also find an argument, which questions this. The continuance of poverty, unemployment, under employment and suicide by the farmers in several States in large numbers virtually defies this argument. There is, therefore, a need for a scientific analysis of the whole development policy and strategy.

The UNDP's Human Development Report 2005 raises quite a few issues which are nothing but alarming so far as India is concerned. Basing on this Report a national daily wrote a thought-provoking editorial.[24] The editorial is titled ' Beyond the Members: India's Welfare Failure is Unique and Shocking'. *The Human Development Report* (HDR) 2005 tells us what we knew all along: The more the world changes the more it remains the same. The HDR also makes disturbing observations on widening disparities between and within rich and poor countries. World trade has increased, but OECD countries still account for two-thirds of all exports. That growing inequality is part of India's reform story is an established fact. What larger lessons do we draw from all this? The fruits of world trade have been redistributed within the poorer countries, with no significant transfer happening from the rich to the poor.

A democracy that offers civil liberties but cannot ensure physical survival, in a country that is not poor anymore, is a curious thing indeed. However, it appears that our political class is waking up to the shame of death and disease.[25] A news item very recently reported a news about farmers seeking mercy killing from the President A.P.J. Abdul Kalam in order to end their owes which they have been suffering for last 20 years.[26] Suicidal deaths by the farmers in the States like Andhra, Karnataka, Maharashtra leave aside the backward States like Bihar, U.P., Madhya Pradesh, Rajashthan, Orissa is so disturbing that can hardly ignore public attention. These are serious concerns which have to be addressed at the highest policy level.

Since the early 90's the Government of India initiated economic reforms and liberalisation of the economy. It resulted in opening up of the economy to the global market. This has consequently affected the earlier nature of Indian State and the process of development as well. How far this change has been for improving the quality of life of teeming million in India is a matter of opinion. It also needs to be examined as to whether liberalisation has served the public interest better than, earlier economic policies. These are the issues that needed a scientific investigation. In view of these problems facing the Indian social order, the present study was proposed. The information gathered and observations made are being presented in the report.

REFERENCES

1. *The Concept of Development: An Issue in the Study of Human Behavior,* (Ed.) Dale B. Harris, University of Minnisote Press, Minnespolis, 1957, p. 3
2. *Ibid.* p.4
3. *Ibid.* pp. 4-5
4. *Ibid.* pp. 5-6.
5. Ibid p.6.
6. *Ibid.* P. 8.
7. *Ibid.* P. 9.
8. *Ibid.* pp. 9-10.
9. *Ibid.* p. 10. This is Dobzhansky, Words to the American Society of Naturalists.
10. *Ibid.* P. 15.
11. *Ibid.*
12. *Culture and Development; Cultural Patterns in Areas of Under Development,* Alexander, K.C. and Kumaran, K.P., Sage Publication, New Delhi, 1962, p. 14.
13. *Society, Culture and Development,* Mukharjee, Ram Krishna, Sage Publication, New Delhi, 1991, p. 88.

14. *Models of Development: A Critique,* Verma J.M.S.; in Development Debate, Srivastava, S.P., Rawat Publication, Jaipur, 1998, p. 39.
15. *Ibid.*
16. *The Development Debate,* Srivastava, S.P., Rawat Publication, Jaipur, 1998, pp.19-20
17. *Ibid,* p. 20.
18. United Nations, Measures for the Economic Development of Under-Developed Countries (New York: United Nations, 1951).
19. The Right to Development in Context, Stephen P Marks in the *Right to Development: A Premier Centre for Development and Human Rights,* Sage Publications, New Delhi, 2004, p. 23
20. *Ibid.*
21. Preamble declares India to be a "Sovereign, Socialist, Secular, Democratic, Republic".
22. *The Development Debate: Critical Perspective,* S.P. Srivastava, Rawat Publications, Jaipur, 1998, p. 2.
23. *Ibid.*
24. *The Times of India,* Lucknow, Sept-9, 2005.
25. *Ibid.*
26. The Times of India, Lucknow, July 17, 2006.

Chapter 2

Methodology and Profile of the Universe

Methodology occupies a prominent place in any form of research. It is on this methodology that the entire research process depends. We, in the social sciences too, give an adequate focus and importance to the methodological preference. Depending upon the needs of the study, methodological tools have to be developed and adopted to give the study a scientific genre. The present study has taken care of these aspects in devising its methodology and the tools.

So far as the time span is concerned, the study focused on the post-independence period which is also a period of planned development in India. Another distinct focus of the study is a pre and post-liberalisation initiated through new economic policy. The study also proposed to assess the level and extent of state intervention in the development process. The main focus of the study, however, will be to examine the post-liberalisation scenario in the country. It will take into account the political, economic and social parameters to form opinion on the theme of the subject. The following are the main objectives of the study.

OBJECTIVES OF THE STUDY

The main objectives of the study are as under:

(i) To assess various strategies and models adopted for socio-economic development in the country.

(ii) To examine the extent and relevance of State intervention in socio-economic development in the country.

(iii) To identify the parameters for the assessment of growth and development.

(iv) To examine the changes effected after the economic reforms initiated in the 90's.

(v) To examine the achievement level in the process of development.

(vi) To suggest changes, if needed, in the contemporary policies and strategies of development.

SCOPE AND METHODOLOGY ADOPTED

With these above objectives the study was undertaken. In order to base its generalisation and opinions, two states, one from the north and the other from the southern region were selected. The states thus, selected were Uttar Pradesh and Karnataka. The study therefore, primarily concerns about state of affairs in these two selected states. Though information about other states have also been made use of. We also got two districts from each state identified and selected for detailed probing and collection of primary data. Data and information from the Block level was also be collected to supplement the available data and information. Effort was thus, made to have the information about the study from different levels in order to have a realistic assessment.

The study made use of both the sources of data i.e. the primary as well as the secondary. The primary source of data was collected through a structured schedule (Annexure – I) prepared for the purpose. Apart from these, interview guides were also drawn for the purpose of interview with senior bureaucrats associated with development policy and planning. The secondary sources consisted of examination of records, files, books and other published material concerned with theme. The study also made use of observation as one of the major tools of data collection.

The data so collected was examined and analysed through computer and necessary quantification has been done for the purposes of analysis. The study on which the book is based, made use of both the deductive as well as survey research method.

PROFILE OF THE UNIVERSE

As stated earlier for the purposes of specific data and information, the two states of Indian Union, i.e. Uttar Pradesh and Karnataka were selected. We now briefly present the profile of these two selected states.

A-1. UTTAR PRADESH

Uttar Pradesh is the biggest state of Indian Union in terms of population, one of the border states in the country and forms a major area of the Northern fertile plain of the Indo-Gangetic plain. Its history is very ancient and interesting. It is recognised in the later Vedic Age as *Brahmarishi Desha* or *Madhya Desha*. Many great sages of the Vedic time like Bhardwaj, Gautam, Vashishtha, Vishwamitra and Valmiki flourished in this State. Several sacred books of the Aryans were also composed here. Two great epics of India, *Ramayana* and *Mahabharat*, appear to have been inspired by Uttar Pradesh. Such is the rich heritage that the State is proud of.

Uttar Pradesh is truly the heart land of India situated in Northern India and share its border with Himanchal, Punjab, Delhi, Madhya Pradesh, Bihar and international border with Nepal. It lies between latitude of 24 degree to 31 degrees and longitude 77 degrees to 54 degrees East. It has an area of 2.94 million square kilometer and area wise rank fourth in the country. As per the 2001 census the state has a population 16.6 crores. Out of these 8.7 crore were males and the rest 7.8 crores were of females. The sex ratio per thousand male has been reported to be 898.

Uttar Pradesh can be divided into 3 distinct hypo-geographical regions:

- The Himalayan region in the North
- Gangetic plain in the Centre
- The Vindhya Hills and Plateaus in the South

The perpetual snows in the higher reaches are the source of perennial rivers and rivulets which criss-cross the terrain and ultimately find their two rivers together with their tributaries form a big river system from a big system which waters the entire Gangetic plain. The traditional belt running along the entire length of the state is called the *terai* and *blabhar* area. The most important area of the economy of the state is the Gangetic plain which stretches across the entire length of the State from east to west.

The entire alluvial plain can be divided into three sub-regions. The first in the eastern track consisting of 14 districts which are subject to periodical floods and droughts and have been classified as scarcity areas. These districts have high density of population which gives the lowest per capita land. The other two regions, the central and western are comparatively better with a well-developed irrigation system. They suffer from water logging and large-scale user tracks.

The Gangetic plain is watered by the Yamuna, the Ganga and its tributaries, the Ram Ganga, the Gomti, the Ghagra and Gandak. The whole plain is alluvial and very fertile. The chief crops cultivated are paddy, wheat, millet, gram, barley, and sugarcane is the chief crops of the region.

CLIMATE

The climate of the State is tropical monsoon, but variations exist because of different altitudes. The average temperature varies in the plain from 3-4 degree Celcius in January to 43-44 degree Celcius in May and June. There are three distinct seasons—the cold season from October to February, summer from March to mid June and the rainy season from mid June to September. Floods are a recurring problem of the State causing damage to crops, life and property. The eastern districts are most vulnerable to floods, the western districts slightly less and the central districts markedly less.

THE PEOPLE

Uttar Pradesh offers a typical example of mini India wherein people belonging to different religions, caste, cultures have been living together. We do not have much interactions on this aspects so far ancient India is concerned, but the medieval, the modern and the post-independent India has enough evidence to substantiate this fact of life of the people of the State. There is another central fact of the social order of Uttar Pradesh and that is the existence of the caste system among the Hindus who constituted the vast majority of the population. This caste hierarchy consists of *Brahmin, Kshatriya, Vashyay* and *Shudras*. The rigid caste attitude in the past and the social and political tensions have resulted in the growth of large settlements of particular castes in compact regions in Uttar Pradesh. Thus there are a large population of *Ahir, Gujars, Kurmi, Bhumihars* and so on in different parts. The Scheduled Caste and the *Harijan* have their own settlement everywhere. The Muslims are not evenly distributed over the state. They are found in western divisions of Meerut, Agra and Rohilkhand and in eastern districts in the *terai* area, in Gonda and Bahraich, Azamgarh, Jaunpur and Ghazipur. The middle class, comparatively thin among Muslims, is engaged in traditional trades, like leather, timber, tobacco and perfume. There is only a sprinkling of Muslims in services and profession.

THE ECONOMIC SCENARIO

The state of Uttar Pradesh is generally considered an economically backward state of Indian Union. It is one of the BIMARU STATES of the region. Agriculture has been the traditional base, though industries of various nature and sizes have been in existence almost all these years. The per capita income of the state at Rs. 4787 in 1993-94 is one of the lowest in the country except Orissa (Rs. 4726) and Bihar (Rs. 3620) the per capita income of the state in 1950's at Rs. 259 was very close to the national per capita income of Rs. 267, short only by Rs. 8, i.e. 3 per cent only. This shows that the state of the economy was a good or bad as that of the nation's economy in the initial years of our independence. It may be worth noting here that the post-1974 period was, marked by a significant empowerment in the total income of the state. The state achieved a grant of 5-7 per cent per annum, which is higher than the national growth of 5-3 per cent. But this again is higher growth rate of total income in the state was lost to the state due to increase in growth rate of population from 1.8 per cent per annum in 1961-71 to 2.3 per cent in 1971-81 which is higher than the country's population growth rate of 2.2 per cent.

The structure of state income shows that the contribution of primary sector has declined to 41 per cent of the state income though the sector still sustain 33 per cent of the total working force. This shows the continued pressure of working population in the primary sector. The share of secondary sector, on the other hand, has gone up to 20 per cent of the total income which now employ 9 per cent of the total workers in the state. This percentage is lowest among all the major Indian states except Bihar (4.6 per cent in 1991), Madhya Pradesh (8.4 per cent in 1991) and Orissa (7.5 per cent in 1991). The share of tertiary sector has been more impressive from 25 per cent in 1970-71 to 37 per cent in 1994-95 and the percentage share of workers employed by this sector has risen from 15 per cent to 18 per cent in 1991. It thus, shows that the UP's growth has been more capital intensive than labour intensive, more urban based than rural based.

The distinguishing features of Uttar Pradesh's economy is its regional imbalances. In terms of economic indicators like agricultural productivity, infrastructural facilities, identical growth, different regions for different levels of development and growth so far as these indicators are concerned. The western region is better placed than the eastern region. This has been the situation almost all through the post-independent period of development in the state.

For administrative purposes the State is divided into 17 divisions, 70 districts and 820 blocks.

A-1 UTTAR PRADESH

In Uttar Pradesh we identified two districts for the purpose of data collection and information on specific issues concerned with the study. The district, thus, identified were Bahraich and Meerut, one from the eastern and the other from the western region of the state. We very briefly present the basic situation of these districts here.

(i) Bahraich

The district of Bahraich lies in sub-Himalayan belt along the border of Nepal and in north-western most district of Faizabad region. Bounded on north and north-east by the territory of Nepal on the east and south-east by Gonda district, on the south and south-west by Barabanki district and on the west by Kheri and Sitapur districts, the districts spread over an area of 6877 sq. km. putting on a shape of an irregular triangle.

The history of the tract that consist Bahraich district is traceable since ancient times. There are references of the area in ancient Indian literature linking with it the hoary past. It is said that this area was developed by Balmiki Rishi. As *Vayu Puran* has it, this area was made capital by Brahma Ji after the creation of the Universe and was known as Gandhar Van. Later on it acquire the name of Brahmaich or 'Assembly of Brahme' which by and by corrupted to Bahraich, bounding this tract was Shravasti, the capital of Uttar Kaushal which was said to have been ruled by Lav, the son of Shri Ram Chandra Ji and which finds references in *Ramayana* and *Mahabharata*. Mentioned in Buddhism and Jainism and the travelogue of Faehin and Huen Tsang Shravasti was not only the capital of an affluent and powerful country but also a center of propagation of

Buddhism. Before Muslim rule, this area was ruled by powerful Bhar dynasty. The archeological remain in the district are said to have belonged to them. It is also said that the name of this area bears its origin to the word Bahraich which means the place of Bhars which later became Bahraich. During the Mughals it became part of Sube-e-Awadh and during the British period the Rajputs of Raikavr and Gangwar lineage held this area under their sway as *Jagirdar.*

The above description shows that the socio-economic and political richness of the area during different phases of its historical development. The contemporary scenario, however, is not that rich. It is rather one of the backward district of the State from various view points. The majority of the population (90 per cent) depends on agricultural which is frequently affected by floods and droughts. Animals husbandry occupies an important place in the agricultural economy of the district. No important mineral deposits are known to occure in the districts. The industrial structure of the districts is weak.

For the administrative purpose the district is divided into three *tehsils* and there are 19 community development blocks through which the development is effected.

(ii) Meerut

Another district selected for our purpose was from the western region i.e. Meerut. It is considered as one of the most important districts from various reasons, one being its nearness to Delhi, the capital of India. The district Meerut (which forms the part of the revenue division of the same name), is named after its headquarters and is said to be associated with earliest traditions of Hindus according to which Maya, the father in law of Ravana founded this place which has therefore, been called Maidut-Ka-Khera. According to another version Maya, a distinguished architect, bought from king Youdhisthir the land on which the city of Meerut now stands and he called this place Mayrasthra, a name which in course of time became shortened to Meerut. Tradition are so has that the district formed part of the dominions of Mahipals, King of Indraprastha and the word Meerut is associated with this name.

Meerut district is the part of the upper Ganga-Yamuna *Doabs*, which lies 28 degree 37′ and 29 degree and 18′ in north direction and 77 degree and 7′ and 78 degree 7′ in east direction. In shape it is roughly rectangular, its length from east to west ranging between 92 Km and 51 Km. from north to south direction. On the north it is bounded by district Muzaffarnagar, on the south by that of Bulandshar district and on the south Ghaziabad and district Bhagpat is in the west direction. Ganga river makes its boundary in east direction separates it from the districts of Moradabad and Bijnore. Hindon river makes its boundary in west direction it separates it with the Bhagpat district.

According to census 2001, the area of the district 2547 Sq. Km. where rural area is 2406 Sq. Km. and urban area is 141.44 sq. km. The total population of Meerut as per census 2001 is 30 million of which 154 million are rural and 146 million are urban. The literacy rate of the district is 65.9 against the national rate of 59 per cent.

For administrative purpose the district has been divided into three *tahsils* namely – Meerut, Mawana and Sardhana. The number of development block in the district stand upto 12. This is the brief profile of the district.

A-2 KARNATAKA

Karnataka is the eighth largest State in India in both area and population. It was formerly known as Mysore. On November 1, 1973, the name of Mysore was changed to Karnataka. It lies between 74^0 and 78^0 East Longitude and, 11^0 and 18^0 north Latitude. It is situated on western edge of the Deccan plateau and is surrounded by Maharashtra and Goa on the north, Andhra Pradesh on the east, and Tamil Nadu and Kerala on the south. On the west it opens out on the Arabian Sea.

The history of Karnataka goes back to the period of epics, the capital of Bali and Sugreeva, 'Monkey King's' of the *Ramayana,* is said to have been Hampi in Bellary district. Vatapi, associated with the sage Agastya, is obviously Badamin in Bijapur district. In the fourth century BC Karnakatka was part of the great Mauryan Empire. Siwanagiri (Kanakagiri in Reichur district) is said to have been the southern capital of the Mauryas.

By the beginning of the sixth century AD, the Chalukyas established a new empire. After the Chalukyas empire, the Yadavas of Devagiri and the Hoysalar of Dwarsamundra divided Karnataka between them. In the 14th century AD the great Vijaynagar empire was established. It was an age of glory and prosperity. A confederation of Muslim Sultans of the Deccan destroyed the Vijaynagar umpire in 1565 (Battle of Talikota). The vast ruins at Hampi, near Horpet, remain today as sombre reminder of the Vijaynagar glory.

In AD 1399 Yaduraya, the ruler of small principality, Mysore, founded the Wodeyar Dynasty. Raja Wodeyar (AD 1578-1612) enlarged the principality into a mighty Kingdom, with Sri Ranga–Patnam as his capital. The Wodeyars were overthrown by Hyder Ali, the intrepid

Muslim General of Mysore. With the defeat of Tipu, the son of Hyder Ali, by the British the Wodeyars were restored to power as a territory of the British. During British rule, the Karnataka area was distributed among the Princely State of Mysore, Hyderabad, and the British provinces of Bombay and Madras and the small principality of Coorg.

The formation of present State represented the fulfillment of the age-old aspirations of Kanada speaking people to come together in a single State. The old kingdom of Mysore formed the nucleus of the new state.

THE PEOPLE

Karnataka is habited by perhaps most cosmopolitan people of the South India. The north of Karnataka is dominated by the Lingayats while in the south, Vokkaligas, a peasant caste, are the most powerful. The largest religious community is that of Hindus. Of the minority religious groups Muslims are the largest community. The others are Christians, Jains and Buddhists.

The total population of the State as per 2001 census is 52,850,562 of which 26,898,918 are male and the rest 25,951,644 are female. The majority of population is living in rural areas. The exact number of people living in rural areas is 34,889,003 and the rest 17,961,529 live in the urban areas. As a major part of the State is rural, the people live a very simple life. The cities, however, present a different picture being more modern, fast and cosmopolitan in nature. Kannad, is the main language spoken, read and written. In urban area one can get by with the knowledge of English and Hindi. As in most States in India, the population there is predominantly Hindu. The people in Karnataka also share a rich cultural heritage. The folk theatre has an ancient and rich tradition. One therefore, gets a rich mix of modernity and tradition, simplicity and fashion co-exists in the land of Karnataka.

CLIMATE

The State enjoys the three main types of climate. The tropical mansoon climate covers the entire coastal belt and adjoining areas. The climate in the region is hot with excessive rainfall during the monsoon season i.e. June to September. The southern half of the State experiences hot, reasonably dry tropical savana climate while most of the northern half experiences hot, semi-arid, tropical steppe type of climates. The climate of the States varies with the season.

THE SEASON

The winter season from January to February, is followed by summer season from March to May. The period from October to December form the post-monsoon season. The period from October to March covering post-monsoon and winter season, is generally pleasant over the entire State except during a few spells of rain associated with north-east monsoon which affects the southern part of the State during October to December.

THE ECONOMIC SCENARIO

Being predominantly a rural and agrarian State, agriculture in Karnataka has always held the center stage of the States' economy. In earlier times Karnataka was famous for its rice, *ragi* and *jowar*, crops and rice was a major export from its coastal ports. Spices like pepper, cardamom, cinnamon, nutmeg, ginger, etc. were also grown in the area in plenty. Later Karnataka unlinked food crops like maize, vegetables like potato and tomato, cash crops like tobacco, long fibred cotton, coffee, and tea, oil seeds like ground nut and spices like chilies from Portugal, England and Latin American countries. Sericulture has resulted in a major agricultural activity in Karnataka.

Agriculture at present is the main source of food for the population and fodder for the cattle. It is the livelihood to around 65 per cent of the population. Agriculture holding, favor implements, irrigation works and livestock represent the largest fixed capital in the State. It can therefore, be seen that inspite of the development in other sectors like IT, Tourism, etc. it is the agriculture which continues to be the mainstay of Karnataka's economy.

The economic scenario includes the industries as well as they also play an important role in the overall development of the State. The government of Karnataka pursuing a progressive Industrial Policy and extending an attracting package of incentives and concession for new industrial investments for more than two decades now. The industrial policy 1996 and the package of incentives and concession, 1996-2001 of Government of Karnataka reflects the governments aspirations on attracting the investment in a liberalised economy. The State Government has also reorganised the need to attract investments in certain important sectors of industries, amongst which agro-based industries have been identified as a "thrust sector" industry for focused attention. The Government has also amended the Land Reforms Act providing for grant of permission to industries for the purchase of agricultural land up to certain extent.

Despite these measures, the Agro-Food Processing Industry sector has not grown to the desired extent. It has, however, been undenibably established that there is vast untapped potential in the State in the sector which would be used advantageously to achieve multiple goals *viz.* rural industrialisation, provision of more hygienic food products, drastic reduction in wastage of primary agricultural – horticultural products, increased export and employment generation. These steps are important to boost the rural economy of the State.

It may be noted that Karnataka, due to its unique agro-climatic conditions, is a major producer of a number of agricultural, horticultural, and plantation crops. It is the largest producer of coffee, second largest producer of fruits and vegetables, a major producer of coconuts, spices and flowers and a significant contributor to the national production to the rice, maize, jowar and a number of food and other crops.

These are the main contributors to the rural economy of Karnataka. In order to sustain the rural economy a policy regarding Agro-Food Processing was also formulated which is considered to be the exclusive industrial promotion policy. This policy has the main objective of initiating and integrated approach to accelerate investment Agro-Food Processing industrial sector. The policy has therefore, addressed all areas right from promoting the production of the appropriate quality of seeds and of the plant materials and covered other important aspects of the sector namely – infrastructure, research and development, human resource development, financial assistance and taxation. It was thus hoped that this policy when implemented could ensure–

(a) Better return to farmers

(b) Elimination or minimisation of wastage of agricultural and horticultural produces.

(c) Production of value added processed food not only for indigenous consumption but also for export,

(d) Availability of nutritious and hygienic food products for general consumption.

(e) Encouragement of investment and employment generation in areas where agriculture is still a predominant activity, and

(f) Provision of appropriate linkages between the agricultural and industrial sectors.

How far these policy initiatives helped the farmers and the economy will be addressed in the chapter that are to follow.

Chapter 3

The Development Scenario

India began its journey of planned development with formal launch of the First Five-Year Plan. The present chapter proposes to analyze the development scenario with plan perspectives. We would therefore, be analysing the perspectives of different Five-Year Plans with a view to see as to how far we have been able to achieve what we wanted to achieve. Further, this chapter would cover a period upto the year 1990 only i.e. upto the Seventh Five-Year Plan. It is thus, an analysis of our planned effort of almost four decades of development planning.

Looking at the approach of the First Five-Year Plan, it had a two-fold objective. Firstly, it aimed at correcting the disequilibrium in the economy caused by the War and the partition of the country. Secondly, it proposed to initiate simultaneously a process of all-round balanced development which would ensure a rising national income and a steady improvement in living standards over a period. While the investment pattern envisaged in the Plan was worked out with due regard to the immediate objective and the resources immediately in sight, the approach to the problem of mobilisation and development of resources was formulated in the light of long-term objectives. It was also emphasised that the aim was not merely to plan within the existing socio-economic framework but to change this framework progressively and by democratic methods in keeping with the large ends of policy enunciated in the Constitution. The First Five-Year Plan was thus, a step in a new direction, a step which invoked greater direct responsibility for the State in promoting development and a greater degree of coordination of development activity in all economic sectors and at all levels.[1] A word may be said here about the instruments and techniques which the report on the first Five-Year Plan dealt with. It was emphasised in that report in the transformation of the economy in the light of the objectives and priorities accepted that state will have to play the crucial role. During the plan period there has been a considerable enlargement of the responsibility of the State in the economic field. While the responsibility for industrial development in the first plan period was placed mainly on the private sector, the State exercised a regulatory role and has endeavored to encourage private investment in priority lines. The role of the state as a key factor in development has come to be fully recognised, whether the state enter the field directly or confine itself to exercise general control and direction. It must, however, be said that the modest scale of investment in the first plan and the improvement in the economic situation consequent on increase in both agricultural and industrial obviated the need on the part of the state to use the techniques of regulation and control with vigour.[2]

It has been observed that the working of the plan has brought out even more clearly than before the need for an improvement in statistical and analytical techniques for the formulation of suitable policies and their assessment. In retrospect it appears that at a certain stage in the Five-

Year Plan period investment could, with advantage, have been stepped up beyond the levels than current.[3] In the overall analysis of the first Five-Year Plan it could be said that the plan was instrumental in bringing about a marked improvement in the levels of production, both in agriculture and in industry. It also initiated a number of structural and institutional changes. The plan has evoked widespread public interest and enthusiasm and these is a new and consistent urge for rapid development all over the country. The first plan was only an initial step.

It could thus, be observed that the First Five-Year Plan was the first step towards the planed development, it covered wide range of activities considered important for nation's growth and development. One could briefly identify the areas like agriculture, industry, co-operatives, animal husbandry, and fisheries, forest and conservation, irrigation and power, village and small industries, transport and communication, education, health, housing, scientific and technological research along with steps towards land reforms. The Plan provided a major thrust to agriculture and alive sector in order to address the problem face by the rural areas. We also witness a new strategy in the shape of community development projects and national extension review programme which were initiated during the plan period for rural development. The first five-year plan therefore, could be considered a landmark in the development effort in post-independent India. It has evoked public co-operation and enthusiasm and has given a new dimension to current thinking and policy.

Our concern is also related to the development perspective for rural India where majority of population lives. In this context it may be noted that community development programme and National Extensive Service programme were initiated during this plan period only with a lot a hope. It provided for a new strategy as well as a new infrastructure for rural development in India. The creation of community development blocks in the year 1952 and then National Extension Service blocks were to serve as new vehicles of development. By the end of the First Five-Year Plan, the community projects and national extension service programme had been taken up in about 1,40,000 villages situated in 988 blocks and was serving a population of 77.5 million people.

The Second Five-Year Plan had to carry forward the process initiated in the first five-year plan period. It had to provide for a larger increase in production, in investment and in employment. Simultaneously it said to accelerate the constitutional change needed to make the economy more dynamic and more progressive in terms no less of social than of economic ends.[4] The Second Plan explains it concerns and elaborates the concept of socialistic pattern of society. A rising standard of life is of course, not an end itself. Essentially, it is a means to a better intellectual and cultural life. A society which has to devote the bulk of its working force on its working hours to the production of the bare where without of life is to that extent limited in its pursuits of higher ends. Economic development is included to expand the country's production power and to provide the environment in which there is scope for the expression and application of diverse faculties and urges. These basic values or basic objectives have recently been summed up in the phrases 'socialistic pattern of society'.[5] The socialistic pattern of society is not to be regarded as something fixed or rigid pattern. It is not rooted in any doctrine or dogma. Each country has to develop according to its own genesis and tradition. Economic and social policy has to shape from time to time in the light of historical circumstances.

Within this broad approach the Second Five-Year Plan was formulated with reference to the following main objectives:[6]

(a) A sizeable increase in national income so as to raise the level of living in the country;

(b) Rapid industrialisation with particular emphasis on the development of basic and heavy industries;

(c) A large expansion of employment opportunities and

(d) Reduction of inequalities in income and wealth and more even distribution of economic power.

The Plan document observed that these objectives are interrelated. A magnificent increase in national income and a marked improvement in living standards cannot be secured without a substantial increase in production and investment. Economic objectives cannot be diverse from social objectives and means and objectives go together. These objectives have to be pursued in a balance way, for expressive emphasis on any one of this may change the economy and delay the realisation of the very objectives which is being stretched.

It is pertinent to note that investment in basic industries creates demands for consumer goods, but it does not enlarge the supply of consumer goods in shorter run; nor does it directly absorbs any large quantities of level. A balanced pattern of industrialisation, therefore, requires a well-organised effort to utilize labour for increasing the supplies of such needed consumer goods in a manner which economises the use of capital. A society in which labour is plentiful in relation to capital has to develop the art and technique of using labour intensive models of production effectively and to much social advantage – in diverse fields. Indeed, in the context of prevailing unemployment, the absorption of labour becomes an important objective in itself. In using labour - intensive methods, it may well be that the cost of the product is somewhat higher. This entails a sacrifice which can be reduced through technical and organisational improvements.[7]

It is worth taking note of the fact that the Constitution of India provided for a specific role for the state in relation to social and economic goals in respect of the people at large. One can refer to the Directive Principles of State Policy which clearly elaborates on that. The Second Five-Year Plan therefore, tries to observe those in the planning process. It tells that the adoption of the socialistic pattern of society as the national objectives, as well as the need for planned and rapid development, requires that all industries of basic and strategic importance, or in the nature of public utility service, should be in the public sector. Other industries which are essential and requires investment on a scale which only the State, is present circumstances could provide, have also to in public sector. The State has, therefore, to assume direct responsibility for future development of industries over a wider area. Never the less, there are limiting factors which make it necessary at this stage for the State to deprive the field in which it will undertake role responsibility for further development, and to make a selection of industries in the development of which it will play a dominant role.[8] This clarification was considered important to avoid cohesion in industrial development sector.

After due consideration and consultation the Government of India decided to classify the industries into three categories, having regard to the part which the State would play in each of them. In the first category will be the exclusive responsibility of the State. The second category will consist of industries, which will be progressively State owned and in which State will therefore generally take the initiative in establishing new undertakings, but in which private enterprise will also be expected to supplement the effort of the State. The third category will include all the remaining industries, and their future development, in general, be kept to the initiation and enterprise of the private sector.[9] The Second Five-Year Plan, therefore, made an expensive policy impact on the future development of the country with a large focus on the industrial sector with a dominant policy initiative for public sector in India.

For rural India the community development programme and national extension service programme were carried out during the Second Five-Year Plan period. In carrying out the programme for this plan period, it is realised that a sense of participation and a definite programme of work for improving its standards of living has to be carried for every rural family. It is hoped that both, through the national extension service and community development programme as well as through other complementary programmes during the next few year, besides agricultural product, there will be marked progress in the following fields:[10]

(i) Development of cooperative activities, including cooperative training;

(ii) Development of *panchayats* as institutions actively responsible for village development;

(iii) Consolidation of holding;

(iv) Development of village and small industries;

(v) Organisation of programmes designed to assist the weaker sections of the village community, specially small farmers, landless tenants, agricultural labourers and artisan.

(vi) More intensive work among women and among youth and

(vii) Intensive work in tribal areas.

As the programme grows in size and the range of activities which it encompasses or influences increase, a great deal of the initiatives in implementing it must pass to the people of each local area. The problem of increasing production and employment and diversifying rural economic life are more complex and will need sustained administrative effort over a considerable period.[11] The Second Plan thus, continued with the experiment of community development and national extension service programme.

There must have been certain lessons drawn after a decade of planed development was completed with the completion of Second Plan. In its scope and emphasis, each five-year plan embodies and assessment of the current economic and social situation and of the progress of the economy over a period of years and at the same time it seeks to relate the next phase of development to the country, basic social objectives and the perspectives of long-term economic growth in drawing up the Third Plan principle aims have been the following:[12]

(i) To secure an increase in national income of over 5 per cent per annum, the pattern of investment being designed also to sustain this rate of growth during subsequent plan periods;

(ii) To achieve self sufficiency in food grain and increased agricultural production to meet the requirements of industry and sports;

(iii) To expand basic industries like steel, chemical industries, fuel and power and establish machine-building capacity, so that the requirements of further industrialisation can be met within a period 10 years or so mainly from the countries own resources;

(iv) To utilize to the fullest possible extent the man power resources of the country and to ensure a substantial expansion in employment opportunities and

(v) To establish progressively greater quality of opportunity and to bring about reduction in disparities in income and wealth and the more even distribution of economy power.

The period of Third Plan represents the first stage of a decade or more of intensive development leading to a self-reliant and self-governing economy. As a result of progress achieved during the first and the second plan the foundation of rapid economic growth have been led. India's economy is now much larger in size and in the large of its operations and has become more dynamic and more complex. In all direction there are a large and growing demand to be met.[13] The general patterns of development followed in a Third Plan necessarily closed, the large part, from the basic approach and its period of the Second Plan. In the theme of development during the Third Plan the first priority necessarily becomes agriculture. Expenses in the first two plans, specially the second, has shown that the rate of growth in agricultural production is one of the main limiting factor in the progress of the Indian economy. Agricultural production has, therefore, to be increased to the largest extent feasible and adequate resources have to be provided under the third plan for realising the agricultural targets.[14] There is a genuine concern expressed in the Third Plan document towards agricultural sector and hence and added focus on increasing agricultural production so as to react the self-suffering level.

The development of basic industries attracted the attention of the Third Plan. It has expressed that development of basic industries such as steel, fuel and power and machine-building and chemical industries is fundamental to rapid economic growth. These industries largely determine the pace at which the economy can become self-reliant and self-generating. Programmes for industrial development have been drawn up from the pint of view of the needs and priorities of the economy as a whole. The public and the private sectors being considered together.[15] The Third Plan, thus, makes an attempt to strike a proper balance between the agricultural and the industrial sector. How far this could be practically achieved, is a matter of time.

In preparing the Third Plan the requirements of the economy as a whole and in different sectors have been considered carefully. The Plan takes into account the results of development over the past 10 years, the increased expectations of the people, the implications of growth in population and of large-scale industrialisation and the need to mobilize the domestic resources of the country to the greater extent possible. It expressed that for achieving a cumulative of growth of 5 per cent per annum; it will be necessary to undertake not investment to the extent of more than 14 per cent of the national income as compared to the present level of 11.5 per cent. This involves raising the rate of domestic saving from about 8.5 per cent to 11.5 per cent by the end of the third plan. Also maintain that dependence at the stage of development on external resources serves to emphasize the importance of policies and measures for import substitution and for increasing export earnings during the Third Plan.[16] It clearly indicates the policy preference of the Third Plan which considers it necessary for the proposed rate of growth during the plan.

So far as the development in the rural sector is concerned the Third plan made its own observation on the basis of the experiences of the earlier two plans. It noted that the community development programme now serves over 3100 development blocks comprising 370,000 villages. Of these about 880 blocks have completed more than five years and entered the second stage of the community development programme. It pointed out that by October 1963, the programme would extend over the entire rural area of the country.[17] This is itself can be considered an achievement.

The second major development concerns the introduction of *Panchayati Raj*. For many years, the establishment of democratic institutions at the district and block levels, in addition to *panchayat* at the village level, was felt to be an essential and inevitable step if rural development was to proceed not only rapidly but largely on the basis of local effort and resources.[18] It may be pointed out here that the recommendation of the Study Team set up by the Committee on Plan Project in favour of a system of democratic decentralisation were considered by the National Development Council on January 1958. The Council affirmed the objectives of introducing democratic decentralisation at the district and block levels and suggested that each state should work out the structure which suited its conditions best. The states, consequently formulated their own enactment to govern the rural areas. This system thus, came to be known as *Panchayati Raj*.

The third aspect of community development work which has assumed significance in the proposal that, along with the district, this block serve as a unit of planning and development.[19] Although efforts were made in several states to prepare block plan especially in agriculture, in the main, the plans of states have been prepared independently of local plans. It can thus, be observed that much more effort will be needed before local plans can become a distinctive stage in the initial preparation of a Five-Year Plan. These three aspects of community development and *Panchayati Raj* are interrelated. This was also the thrust of the third five-year plan.

The Plan further elaborates that the introduction of *Panchayati Raj* raises the wider question of the reorganisation of districts administration. It is not generally realised that over the past decade changes in district administration have been somewhat haphazard.[20] When the community development programme was taken up, the extension organisation had to be superimposed on the traditional district administration without adequate connecting links. In the nature of things, there is still a considerable overlapping which cause for some majors of rationalisation in district also and fresh definition of function and relationship.[21] It is important to note that the third plan while suggesting the new policy initiatives at the district and block level also hinted at the shortcomings which need to be addressed for a better realisation of development goals of rural India.

The three Five-Year Plans implemented so far addressed themselves specially to the problems which emerged either because of new political and economic development in the country and in the world or as a consequence of progress already achieved. The priority and the emphasis have necessarily changed and have had to be adjusted from Plan to Plan. The Fourth Plan thus, represents a conscious, internally consistent and carefully thought out programme for the most efficient exploitation of our resources possible in existing conditions.

The Fourth Five-Year Plan had to provide the next step forward in attaining accepted aims and objectives of Indian planning. It expresses that in formulating it, note has to be taken of the success and failures so far, the observed continuing trends in the economy and the specific experiences of recent years. The most notable lesson in that the current tempo of economic activity is insufficient to provide productive employment to all, extend the base of social service and bring about significant improvement in living standards of the people.[22] The Fourth Plan aims at acceleration of the tempo of development in conditions of stability and reduced uncertainties. It is proposed to introduce safeguards against the fluctuation of agricultural production as well as the uncertainty of foreign aid in the period of the Fourth Plan. Together with programme of increased agricultural production, the Plan provides for the building of sizeable buffer stocks to even out the supplies of food grain and other measures to establise food grain prices and the price level in general.[23] It was argued that national self-reliance and growth with stabling can be attained only if additional effort is put forward at every level. It is planned to do away with concessional imports of food grain under PL 480 by 1971. These measures which seek to limit the extent of foreign aid to avoid inflationary financing have influenced the total investment outlay proposed in the Plan.[24]

The projection of real income in 1973-74 in the Fourth Five-Year Plan (1969-74) is appreciably below that implied in the long-term projections outlined in the Third Plan. Both the Second and Third Plan envisaged a doubling of per capita real income in the course of nearly twenty years. The expectation of population growth at the time of formulation of the Third Plan was at higher than assumed in the Second Plan. The higher growth rate of 6 per cent envisaged in the long-term perspective of the Third Plan were meant to offset the effect of the observed faster rate of growth of population. However, for a variety of reasons, the progress of the economy has suffered a set back in recent years.[25] These needed to be addressed.

The Fourth Plan also made an observation that the population growth is an important variable determining the rate of improvement in per capita income. Expressing concern over the rate of the population growth, it had observed that population growth on this scale can be a crippling handicap since our population in relation to resources is already large, incomes are low and economic development in a desperate need. The speed at which a country develops depends largely upon its ability to direct a larger part of its growing resources to investment rather than current consumption. A growing population with a high proportion of dependent children will find it increasingly difficult to do so.[26] The Fourth Plan thus, raised its concern towards the growing population which has its adverse impact on the growth process.

In the sphere of rural development through community development and *Panchayati Raj* system, the working of the programme has thrown up a variety of experiences. The operation of the Block in five year stages, with tempering financial provision from stage to stage, was based on the assumption that, by the end of the initial ten year period, there would be adequate mobilisation of resources by the local institutions and sufficient channeling of other Plan funds to make any separate provision there after for the Block unnecessary.[27] The Plan further observed that with all their drawbacks, the community development programme and *Panchayati Raj* institutions have provided a new dimension to rural development and introduced a structural change of considerable importance the district administration within the limitations of resources the programme has attempted to do something which in any case, had never before been attempted. Improvement of agriculture has remained in forefront through out. During the Fourth Five-Year Plan, therefore, most of the schemes and programmes were continued.

The Fifth Five-Year Plan reviewed the progress of planned development in the country in various sectors of the economy and tried to adjust the problems faced so far in the current exercise. The Fifth Plan covers a period from 1975 to 1979. This is also a period when the country have to face challenges of various kinds. Emergencies of Jai Prakash Narayan on the national political sense with his dictum of 'total revolution' provided a forum for most of the political parties opposed to Congress to come together. All this was going on and internal Emergency was declared by Mrs. Gandhi in the year 1975. This continued for couple of years when the general election was declared in the country and Janta Party came to power with Mr. Morar Ji Desai as the Prime Minister. However, this government did not last the full-term and mid term elections were declared in 1980 in which Mrs. Gandhi again returned to power with a comfortable majority. The fifth Five-Year Plan period has seen various contradictory forces which tried to influence the socio-political as well as the economic scenario in the country. But the fifth plan successfully withstood these adverse influences and went ahead with its strategy and the perspectives towards development. It may be worth noting at this juncture the development programme of various five-year plans. The following table gives targeted and actual growth rates from the first to fifth Five-Year Plan in the country.[28]

Table 3.1

TARGETTED AND ACTUAL GROWTH RATE

Sl. No.	*Plan*	*Target*	*Actual*	*Growth rate for*
1	*2*	*3*	*4*	*5*
1	First Plan	2.1	3.6	National Income
2	Second Plan	4.5	4.0	National Income
3	Third Plan	5.6	2.2	National Income
4	Fourth Plan	5.7	3.3	Net Domestic Product
5	Fifth Plan	4.4	5.2	Gross Domestic Product

Note: Targets were generally specified in terms of net national income/ product upto the fifth plan in which for the first time targets were specified in terms of gross domestic product.

The figures given in the table above clearly indicate the gap between the target and the achievement during various five-year plans. Except the first and the fifth, where it has shown an increase in the actual, other Five-Year Plans fall short of the target. This can, therefore, be observed that in an overall analysis the plan development could not achieve what it wanted to achieve. This is the state of development in almost twenty five years of our planned effort. The continuance of poverty, unemployment, lack of infrastructure, etc. asked for renewed look towards a strategy for planed development. In this context it is worth noting that sixth five-year plan has been formulated against the background of a perspective covering a period of 15 years from 1980-81 to 1994-1995. This development perspective utilises accelerated progress towards the removal of poverty, generation of gainful employment and technological and economic self-reliance.[29] The strategy to attain these goals has been chosen after considering variety of feasible alternative development profits with their attendant costs and benefits.[30] It is in the light of this consideration that the objectives of the sixth plan have been formulated. These objectives are given below. Along with the objectives are also listed major areas of effort which will be required to fulfill these objectives.[31]

1. A significant step in the rate of growth of the economy, the promotion of efficiency in the use of resources and improved productivity.
2. Strengthening the inputs of modernisation for the achievement of economic and technological self-reliance.
3. A progressive reduction in the incidence of poverty and unemployment.
4. A speedy development of indigenous source of energy with proper emphasis on conservation and efficiency in energy use.
5. Improving the quality of life of public in general with special reference to the economically and socially handicap population through minimum needs programme whose coverage is so designed as to ensure that all parts of the country attain within a prescribed period nationally acceptable standards.
6. Strengthening the re-distributive bias of public policies and services in favour of the poor contributing to a reduction in inequalities of income and wealth.
7. A progressive reduction in regional inequalities in the pace of development and in the diffusion of technological benefits.
8. Promoting policies for controlling the growth of population through voluntary acceptance of the small family norms.

9. Bringing about harmony between the short and long-term goals of development by promoting the protection and improvement of ecological and environmental assets, and
10. Promoting the active involvement of all sectors of the people in the process of development through appropriate education, communication and institutional strategies.

The strategy adopted for the sixth plan consisted essentially in moving simultaneously to strengthen the infrastructure for both agricultural and industry so as to create conditions for an accelerated growth in investments, output and exports and to provide, through special programmes, designed for the purpose, increased opportunities for employment specially in the rural areas, and the unorganised sector and meet the basic needs of the people.[32] The attack on the problem of poverty is most affective only in the conditions of an expanding economy. Since growth by itself may not, however, suffice, other programmes and policies will need to be adopted with specific aim of improving the living conditions of the masses and to bring about reduction in inequalities of income and wealth.[33] The Sixth Plan, therefore, clearly sets up its own objective and strategy to register growth and also aim at directly attacking on the problem of poverty and unemployment.

The Sixth Five-Year Plan further proposed to strengthen the process of democratic decentralisation. Irrespective of whatever structural pattern that is existent or that may be devised, effort will be to devolve on these institutions all such functions appropriate to each level, which are capable of being planned and implemented at that level. These institutions will be particularly involved in at that level. These institutions will be particularly involved in the planning and execution of Integrated Rural Development Programme and the National Rural Employment Programme.[34] The *Panchayati Raj* institutions, therefore, continued to play an important role in the rural development process at the district and below.

The Sixth Plan made another attempt towards the structural change in the sphere of rural development administration. It may be noted that District Rural Development Agencies were created in the year 1980 during the Sixth Plan Period with some specific objectives. We have already noted the importance of *Panchayati Raj* institutions in the planning and implementation of rural development programmes. The creation of DRDA, marks another departure from the earlier plan perspective. It was proposed to create these institutions for the purposes of overseeing the planning and implementation of centrally sponsored schemes and programme. It was expressed that if effective programme design is critical to successful implementation of rural development programmes so is an effective delivery agency. None of the anti poverty programmes can have an impact unless they are implemented with a clarity of purpose and commitment to task. It is here that the DRDAs play a critical role. This, in a sense, negates the effort which has already gone in planning and execution through *Panchayati Raj* organisations.

Here the DRDA is visualised as a specialised and a professional agency capable of managing the antipoverty programmes of the Ministry of Rural development on the one land and to effectively relate these to the over all effort of poverty eradication in the district. In other words, while the DRDA will continue to watch over and ensure effective utilisation of the funds intended for anti-poverty programmes, it will need to develop a far greater understanding of the process necessary for poverty alleviation. The role of DRDA, will therefore, be distinct from all other agencies, including the *Zila Parishad*. They are rather expected to coordinate with the line departments, the *Panchayati Raj* institutions, the bank and other financial institute, NGOs, as well as the technical institutions, with a view to gathering the support and resources required for poverty reduction effort in the district.

The DRDAs were expected to coordinate effectively with the *Panchayati Raj* institutions. It was also directed that under no circumstances will they be performing the functions of *Panchayati Raj* institutions. They will maintain their separate identity but will function under the chairman of the Zila Parishad. They are expected to be a facility and supporting organisation of the Zila Parishad keeping in view the substantial investment that are being made in poverty alleviation programme, the DRDAs shall ensure financial discipline in respect of funds received by them whether from the Central or State Government. Thus, the role of the DRDA is in term of planning for effective implementation of anti-poverty programmes, coordinate with other agencies enabling the community and the rural poor to participate in the decision making process overseeing the implementation to ensure adherence to guidelines. However, the role of DRDA was confined to antipoverty programmes.

Now the programme of development during the seventh plan, it was affirmed, must be set against the perspectives of the next fifteen years: 1985-2000. The investment programmes and the policy initiatives for the Seventh and the subsequent plans must be related to the goals that the nation has far the year 2000, as it emerges into the 21st century. In more than concrete terms this means the elimination of poverty and creating conditions of near full employment, satisfaction of basic needs of the people in terms of food, clothing and shelter, attainment of universal elementary education and access to health facilities for all.[35] In the sphere of industry, efficiency must be progressively improved so as to attain international competitiveness in major products. The aim should be to make India a modern, technologically progressive economy with expanding capacity to provide the basic material and cultural requisites of well being for all people. The attainment of all these goals requires:[36]

i) Action to sustain and enhance to momentum the economic expansion and technological development;
ii) Adoption of effective promotional majors to raise the productivity and the income of the poorer section of the population, poorer regions and poorer states;
iii) Expansion and qualitative improvement in facility for health, education and other basic civic amenities;
iv) Majors for bringing about a sharp reduction in the rate of population growth.

It was argued that the Seventh Plan must built on the strength inherited from the part – the high rate of growth, the large pool of scientific, technological and managerial manpower, the resilience against drought and international disturbances and the orientation of the development effort to benefit the poor. It is now possible to move faster towards the objective of self-sustaining growth with social justice.[37] The objective of the Plan was to sustain and accelerate the growth rate with the experiences of the earlier Plans.

The long-term strategy for the Seventh Plan was to take into account the objective conditions in the economic and the likely developments over the planning horizon. The Plan made it clear that the demographic perspective should be taken at the starting point for determining a long-term development strategy. The persons who will join the labour force in the next fifteen years have already been born. In absolute terms, around 120 million persons will be added to labour force over the next 15 years. Thus, creation of opportunities for productive employment of a growing labour assumes top priority. Further, agriculture sector has its own role in the economy. The increasing demand for food in the process of growth favourable income and employment implication of more intensive agricultural development and the severity of balance of payments constraint requires that continued fast agricultural growth and self-suffering in food must remain a top priority concern of planning in India.[38] The Plan therefore, argues for a strategy which could generate more employment as well as focus on increased agricultural growth.

The Seventh Plan while summing up its strategy for the period explained that it aims at a direct attack on the problems of poverty, unemployment and regional imbalances. It requires for its success substantial improvement and economy in resource base.[39] There is therefore, little change so far as the strategy is concerned as the Sixth Plan too advocated for a direct attack on poverty and unemployment and initiated programmes like the IRDP and NREP.

So far as the planning and implementation of rural development programmes at the district and below are concerned the Seventh Plan made its observation. The Plan argued that the need for decentralisation of planning and development administration below the State level have been recognised for sometime, particularly in the context of agriculture and rural development programme. But the ideas relating to decentralised planning have been somewhat nebulous and the progress in the various States somewhat halting. Though *Zila Parishads* and *Panchayat Samitis* have been established in several States the actual decentralisation of political and administrative authority has been generally of limited nature. The lack of adequate machinery for decentralised planning and administration, thus, constitutes to be a critical weakness in the existing system.[40] In this context its worth noting that a working group set up by the Planning Commission on district planning in 1982, advocated a gradual, step by step approach towards decentralising the planning process. It has suggested that Panchayati Raj Institutions (PRI), wherever, these exist, will function as the apex body to approve as well as review the implementation of district plans.[41] The recommendation of the working group in a sense, strengthened the position of official hierarchy including the Collector.

During the Seventh Plan period, the decentralisation of the planning process and full public participation in development will be pursued on the lines suggested by the working group which meant that the district Collector had an increased role in this process. These steps, it was hoped, will seek to ensure the achievement of the twin objectives of effective implementation of the anti poverty programmes and ensuring a balanced regional development at least in respect of the minimum needs.[42] There seems to be a clear focus of the Plan so far as the implementation of the rural development programmes are concerned.

We have thus, covered a period of four decades of planned development in India i.e. from 1951 to 1990, a period covered through seven Five-Year Plans. We have seen the priorities, strategies, policies and the programmes formulated and implemented during these four decades. Let us briefly look at the growth achieved in different sectors under various five-year plans. The following tables gives figures of the same.

Table 3.2

GDP GROWTH, RATES FOR INVESTMENT AND INCREMENTAL CAPITAL OUTPUT RATIO (ICOR) IN INDIAN ECONOMY (1951-1990)

S.No.	*Period*	*Growth in GDP at Factor Cost %*	*Investment Rate %*	*ICOR*
1	*2*	*3*	*4*	*5*
1.	1951-52 to 1955-56	3.61	10.66	2.95
2.	1956-57 to 1960-61	4.27	14.52	3.40
3.	1961-62 to 1965-66	2.84	15.45	5.44
4.	1966-67 to 1970-71	4.66	15.99	3.43
5.	1971-72 to 1975-76	3.08	17.87	5.80
6.	1976-77 to 1980-81	3.24	21.47	6.63
7.	1981-82 to 1985-86	5.06	20.98	4.15
8.	1985-86 to 1989-90	5.81	22.70	3.91
9.	1985-86 to 1991-92*	5.31	23.17	4.36

Note: Estimates are based on the New Series of National Accounts Statistics, Central Statistical Organisation.

* The average growth rate, investment rate and ICOR for a seven year period (1985-86 to 1991-92) has been worked out by including the estimates of growth and investment rate for 1990-91 as reported in the Quick Estimates of CSO (release in Feb. 1992), and by assuming a growth rate of 2.5% for 1991-92 (as projected in Economic Survey 1991-92).

(**Source:** Eighth Five-Year Plan, Planning Commission, Govt. Of India, New Delhi, Vol. 1, p 3)

Given the structure of the Indian economy, the growth in the national income has largely been determined by the trends in agriculture production. The reason being that

Table 3.3

SECTORAL GOWTH IN GROSS DOMESTIC PRODUCT

(Percent per annum, based on GDP series at 1980-81 prices)

S. No.	Sector	1951-52 to 1955-56	1956-57 to 1960-61	1961-62 to 1965-66	1966-67 to 1970-71	1971-72 to 1975-76	1976-77 to 1980-81	1981-82 to 1985-86	1985-86 to 1989-90
1	Agriculture	2.88	3.35	-0.28	5.36	2.33	1.33	3.16	3.59
2	Mining and Quarrying	4.40	6.96	6.76	1.31	5.38	4.53	6.91	7.03
3	Manufacturing	5.84	6.28	6.62	3.96	3.33	4.86	6.99	6.72
	3.1 Registered	6.18	8.24	8.34	4.67	2.39	5.28	8.56	6.30
	3.2 Unregistered	5.62	4.38	4.60	3.16	4.61	4.39	4.88	7.41
4	Electricity Gas & Water Supply	8.68	12.00	12.84	9.54	6.83	6.91	8.41	9.60
5	Construction	6.80	6.70	6.83	4.36	1.47	5.11	3.36	4.06
6	Trade Hotels & Restaurants	4.79	5.77	5.39	4.22	4.10	4.49	5.96	6.57
7	Transport Storage & Communications	4.38	6.99	6.27	4.72	6.54	5.78	6.81	8.04
8	Financing, Etc.	3.12	2.83	3.31	3.54	3.61	4.56	6.39	8.27
9	Public Admn. & Defense	3.45	6.83	8.97	6.83	4.89	5.89	6.76	8.69
10	Other Services	2.79	3.32	4.24	3.61	2.95	3.00	4.56	6.12
	Total	**3.61**	**4.27**	**2.84**	**4.66**	**3.08**	**3.24**	**5.06**	**5.81**

(**Source:** Eighth Five Year Plan, Planning Commission, Govt. of India, Vol I, p 4.)

agriculture is the largest component of GDP and has overall impact on other sectors in a input linkage, employment and income. This can be seen in the Table 3.3.

It has been argued that manufacturing will occupy a crucial position in future economic development. The nations' ability to grow fast, export, be competitive and credit on expanding base for direct and indirect growth of productive employment would depend upon the growth efficiency of manufacturing sector. After a good start in the Second and Third Plan, the growth performance of the manufacturing sector declined during the late sixties and the seventies, but picked up again during the eighties (Table 3.3).

These four decades of planned development give us a mixed bag of success and failures, if we go deep into the problem facing the nation. The problems in terms of poverty, unemployment, health and education continue to bother the policy planners and the economists at large. Inspite of various programmes and sustained efforts, we have not been able to achieve to the extent we wanted to. The story of state intervention in the development process raised a debate. The fall out of this debate can be seen in the paradigm shift towards the philosophy of development itself. The liberalisation of economic policy and globalisation were perhaps steps in the direction of limiting the state intervention in development. Analysis of the aspects concerned with this shift in development paradigm is being taken up in the following chapter.

REFERENCES

1. Review of the First Five-Year Plan, Planning Commission, Government of India, 1957, p. 1.
2. *Ibid.* p. 12.

3. *Ibid.* p. 3.
4. The Second Five-Year Plan, Planning Commission, Govt. of India, New Delhi, 1956, p. 1-2.
5. *Ibid.* p.p. 21-22.
6. *Ibid.* p. 24.
7. *Ibid.* p. 25.
8. *Ibid.* p. 45.
9. *Ibid.* pp. 45-46.
10. *Ibid.* p. 243.
11. *Ibid.* p. 245.
12. The Third Five-Year Plan, the Planning Commission, Govt. of India, New Delhi, 1961, p. 48.
13. *Ibid.*
14. *Ibid.* p. 49.
15. *Ibid.* p. 5.
16. *Ibid.* p. 51.
17. *Ibid.* p. 332.
18. *Ibid.* p. 333.
19. *Ibid.* p. 334.
20. *Ibid.* p. 341.
21. *Ibid.* pp. 341-342.
22. The Fourth Five-Year Plan, Planning Commission, Govt. of India, New Delhi, p. 13.
23. *Ibid.*
24. *Ibid.* p. 14.
25. *Ibid.* p. 30.
26. *Ibid.* p. 32.
27. *Ibid.* p. 228.

28. Sixth Five-Year Plan, Planning Commission. Govt. of India, New Delhi, p. 1.
29. *Ibid.* p. 17.
30. *Ibid.*
31. *Ibid.* p 34.
32. *Ibid.*
33. *Ibid.*
34. *Ibid.* p. 176.
35. The Seventh Five Year Plan, Planning Commission, Govt. of India, New Delhi, Vol I, p. 7.
36. *Ibid.*
37. *Ibid.* p. 6
38. *Ibid.* p. 7
49. *Ibid.* p. 24
40. *Ibid.* pp. 402-403
41. *Ibid.* p. 403
42. *Ibid.* p. 404

Chapter 4

The Paradigm Shift

There has been a defined role of the state in India's economic development right from the days our effort began towards planned development. The nature of our political economy perhaps necessitated an approach wherein state played a major role in economic development. We opted for a mixed economy model and a socialistic pattern of society initially. Before the coming of the Economic Reform of the 90s, we were through with seven Five-Year Plans which define the goals of development and influenced the destiny of millions of Indians living particularly in the rural areas. There were question marks on the strategies followed for the economic emancipation and the models adopted for the purpose during these four decades of planed development. It can however, be safely observed that the results of the development policies and programmes provided a mixed bag of success and failure.

In the meanwhile the country has started feeling the pressure of the economic reforms taking place across the world. The new economic policy of liberalisation, privatisation and globalisation has its own share of influence on the economies of the third world countries including India. Consequently, a marked shift of focus could be witnessed in our economic policies of the reforms of the 90s. The present chapter proposes to look into shift of focuses and assess as to how far the shift has affected the socio-economic profile of India, particularly rural India.

One can find works highlighting the paradigm shift in rural development particularly. It may be pertinent to note here similar efforts which would provide direction to this debate of paradigm shift. There are studies which have tried to briefly identify the items in the old paradigm and then the exercise in new paradigm. Let us have a look into these two sets of paradigms.[1]

One can identify more than a dozen items which Andrew Shephered has tried to analyze in the context of paradigm shift. We would take some of these for the purposes of analysis in the context of India. Also, we shall be taking these concepts with some appropriate modifications in the context of planning strategy before and after the economic reforms were introduced in the country.

Before attempting this analysis, it may be mentioned here that we have reviewed the development strategies, policies and models pursued through different Five-Year Plans and have tried to look into the extent of impact they have met on the socio-economic life of the people at large. We would now propose to briefly analyze the development scenario in the selected States for the study, namely, the States of U.P. and Karnataka. We however, would like to confine our observation and analysis to rural development and see as to how far our development efforts have yielded results. This analysis would be based, apart from other source material, the information collected through the structured schedules prepared for the purpose and the observation during the course of our study. The analysis

Table 4.1

A SUMMARY OF THE PARADIGM SHIFT

The old paradigm	*The new paradigm*
Economic growth at all costs	Quality growth: environment- enhancing, socially just and acceptable; contributing to peace
Redistribution, if any, by the State	Process of inclusion of the excluded in decisions
Authoritarianism tolerated as price of growth	Intangibles valued: freedom, autonomy, dignity
Subsidies for small enterprises, provided by the State	An 'enabling environment' for enterprise growth
State-provided social (and other forms of) security	Local institutional development for security
Transfer of technology from rich countries	Value local technology and knowledge; participatory technology development
Transfer of valuable assets (eg. genetic resources) to rich countries	Institutions to protect assets of poor communities
Tangible, economic valuation of development: governments to define it	Development as multi-faceted, and often intangible: people to define it
Private/nationalise common properties	Affirm common properties as common, and expand field of goods seen as common
Build large powerful organisations for development: focus on government and large NGOs	Polycentric institutional arrangements: people's organisations, frameworks of governance
Planning = central thought process	Evaluation = central thought process
Organisation hierarchical: to implement plans	Non-hierarchical learning organisation
Compartmentalised	Holistic
Role of the State: major producer, provided and regulator	Role of the State: creating enabling legal frameworks, devolving power, encouraging associations

will cover the area like agriculture, employment, rural health, industry, poverty eradication programmes, etc. which have a direct bearing on the socio-economic life of the people of the area.

The Eighth Five-Year Plan (1992-97) was being launched at a time when the Economic Reforms has already been initiated in the country. It already had started to influence the public policy arena. We have, therefore, to look into the Plan priorities and strategies of the Plan in order to understand as to how it tried to address the issues of 'old paradigm' as well as providing for a 'new paradigm'. In this context it may be pertinent to note the observations made by the then Prime Minister Mr. P.V. Narsimha Rao. He sad that "there is, however, one danger which we must recognize and guard against in the opening up" process. This could lead to wider disparities within the society. To meet this situation, we have to enable the under privileged sections also to derive the benefits of the new opportunities. This process would naturally need some time to fructify. Until that happens, there has to be a by-pass arrangement whereby benefits reach the lowest rungs of the social pyramid directly from the State. We are doing this.[2] These remarks of the Prime Minister during the launching of the Eighth Five-Year Plan, clearly indicates the Plan priorities and sets the tone for economic reform as well.

For various plausible reasons the Eighth Plan desired to orient some of the development paradigm, since its objectives is to lay a sound foundation. For higher growth and to achieve the most significant goals, namely, improvement in the levels of living, health and education of the people, full employment, elimination of poverty and a planned growth in population.

The Eighth Plan is being launched at a time which marks a turning point in both international and domestic economic environment. All over the world centralised economies are disintegrating. On the other hand, economies of several regions are getting integrated under a common philosophy of growth, guided by the market forces and liberal policies. The emphasis is on autonomy and efficiency induced by competition. We cannot remain untouched by these trends.[3] It was further argued that we have to draw lessons from the development experience of other nations during the last four decades. Development economies were largely theoretical when India started for planning in 1951. It has now acquired considerable empirical knowledge based on rich applied experience of many nations, among whom there are success stories as also failures. Indian planning needs to draw on some of these lessons.[4] We shall be looking into these aspects gradually as the discussion procedes further.

The economists have favoured the growth model for quite some time not only in India but across the world. The Indian economy, which was stagnant during the first half of the 20th century, started growing after the launching of the Five-Year Plans. However, the growth rate in Gross Domestic Product (GDP) remained lower than expected and lowered around 3.5 per cent per annum. Even the higher rates of growth (6.8% in the Eighth Plan) have not been able to address the problem facing the Third World countries. This growth model may have had some success in the initial decades of our planned effort. But, people have started questioning this growth. One would like to mention Mahbub-ul-Haq who was a leading economist representing the concern of the Third world. In his book he clearly comes out with the argument that growth has been without justice and therefore, he addressed this as a 'sin' wherein he had identified seven 'sins' of development.[5] He was, however, writing before the Economic Reforms were initiated. This, in a sense, questioned the earlier premises of development paradigms where the State intervention was the major thrust.

The Ninth Five-Year Plan (1997-2002) was launched in the 50th year of India's Independence with the hope that it will take India into the new millennium. The Approach Paper to the Ninth Five-Year Plan had accorded priority to agriculture and rural development with a view to generating adequate productive employment and eradication of poverty, accelerating the growth rate of the economy with stable prices; ensuring food and nutritional security for all, particularly the vulnerable section of society; providing the basic minimum services of safe drinking water, primary health care facility, universal primary education, shelter, connectivity to all in a time bound manner; containing the growth rate of population; ensuring environmental sustainability of the development process through social mobilisation and participation of people at all levels; empowerment of women and socially disadvantaged groups such as Scheduled Castes, Scheduled Tribes and Other Backward Classes and Minorities as agents of social change and development; promoting and developing peoples' participation bodies like *Panchayati Raj* institutions, Cooperative and self-help groups, and strengthening efforts to build self-reliance. These very priorities constitute the objectives of the Ninth Plan.[6] These listed priorities and objectives of the Ninth Plan seem to be well intentioned, but one feels rather skeptical when one looks around the quantum and complexities of the problem being faced by the nation at large, particularly the rural poor.

Indian's development strategy, like that of most of other developing countries, has evolved over successive Plan periods, reflecting the growing strength of the economy, structured transformation taking place in the domestic economy and also development in the world economy. In the early stages of development planning, Government was viewed as the principal actor in development exercising strict control over private investment, ensuring a dominant role of the public sector in all important industries. Trade policy tended to be inward oriented focusing on industrial development through import substitution which was encouraged through a tight control over imports and maintenance of high tariffs. The limitation of this strategy became evident by the end of 1970 and early 1980, while Government was over-active in industries, it was under-active in many areas, specially relating to social development.[7] It was argued at various levels that the development efforts are not getting reflected in many areas of our social development. Some had also started doubting the usefulness of the strategy being followed.

Subsequently, we find some efforts being made to reform the system in the second half of the 1980's to address the shortcomings in our development strategy. However, it was not until 1991 that a wide ranging progress of economic reforms aimed at decontrolling and debureaucratising the economy was initiated. There is no doubt that the Indian economy has responded well to change in policy direction and the growth rate increased from 5.8% in the Seventh Plan to 6.8% in the Eighth Plan. And yet there are many dimensions in which performance has lagged behind expectation.[8] It may be noted that faster growth rate has not reduced poverty as much as it should have, nor has it created the number of high quality jobs we need to satisfy the aspirations of our increasingly educated youths. Growth has not been as regionally balanced as it should have been. The deficiency in social development indicators have also continued and our low level of social development is today a major constraint in reaching a growth rate of 8 per cent which is the mid-term target.[9] This is another issue as to whether even by achieving a growth rate of 8 per cent then we shall be able to address adequately the social development targets.

A logical argument is advanced in favour of reforms to continue. It is being advocated that there should be no doubt that the process of reforms which has been underway for some years, and which has yielded many good results, must continue and be strengthened. The reforms involve a major re-orientation of the role of the State. Instead of being a pervasive controller of private sector activity, and also a direct producer in many areas through majority owned public sector enterprises, the State must play a different role in future.[10] This can be considered a shift in the nature and the function of the State. The Ninth plan proposed an argument for a new paradigm. However, even arrangement of the private sector and reliance upon competitors and market forces does not mean that the State has no role to play or over that its role in development may be reduced. What is involved is not so much a reduction in the role of the State as a re-orientation.[11] How far this re-oriented role of the State has been able to re-orient the developmental ethos, is an issue which we will try to assess in the pages that follow.

It may be worth noting here the areas of special importance for State intervention. The concern expressed about various sectors of public importance is quite similar. In this we can note the concerns about agriculture. It is argued that agricultural sector has historically played an extremely important role in providing employment in India, and is likely to continue to do so at least for the next decade or more. The evidence strongly suggests that small farmer agriculture, based on secure rights on the land, is not only more production per unit of land than either large farm or where the rights of the actual tiller are not well defined, but is also more labour absorbing.[12] This indicates the concern of the planners about the agricultural sector with reference to re-orientation of the role of the State in development process. The paradigm shift proposed and being implemented then, makes us believe that the State intervention in rural development will not be affected and the State will continue to look into the welfare aspects of the rural people.

The end of the Ninth Plan marks the beginning of the twenty first century whereas the Tenth Plan (2002-2007) almost begins its exercise in the new millennium. It may be noted here that the last decade of the 20th Century has been a visible shift in the focus of development planning from the mere expansion of production of goods and services, and the consequent growth of per capita income, to planning for enhancement of human well being. Specific focus on these dimensions of social development is necessary because experience shows that economic prosperity, measured in terms of per capita income, alone does not always ensure enrichment in quality of life, as reflected, for instance, in the social indicators on health, longevity, literacy and environmental sustainability. The development process must therefore, be viewed in terms of the efficiency with which it uses and economises production capacities, involving both physical and human resources, to attain the desired economic and social ends.[13] With these perspectives the Tenth Plan was launched.

Inspite of the efforts of the successive Plans, the problems continued to bother our economic planners. It was mentioned that the limitations that are placed by land and water availability on agricultural output and deployment necessitate careful consideration of the alternatives. It is becoming increasingly clear that the solution would have to found by increasing productivity in agriculture, including agro-forestry, horticulture, animal husbandry and fisheries and by creating employment opportunities in other activities.[14] One can argue that successive Plans have focused on these four areas, but somehow or the other ground realities do not match the Plan perspective.

It has further been observed that the economic and social development of the country must also take full cognigance of all indicators. Not only have the per capita incomes in various States of the Union started diverging rapidly during the past decade, the disparities in social attainments also appear to be persistent. These trends indicate a growing polarisation of the country which can have an extremely damaging affect on national unity and harmony.[15] These are the concerns expressed by the Tenth Plan document which need to be addressed sooner than later.

The Approach Paper had proposed that the Tenth Plan should aim at an indicative target of 8% average GDP growth for the Plan period. It is certainly an ambitious target, especially in view of the fact that GDP growth has decelerated to below 6% at present. The Approach Paper also reorganised that economic growth can not be the only objective of national planning and indeed, over the years, development objectives are being defined not just in terms of increases in GDP or per capita income not have broadly in terms of enhancement of human well-being.[16] This in a sense indicates a change in perception to assess and evaluate the development and its impact. The new approach provides us with the tool of Human Development Index (HDI) as against GDP to assess the growth and development.

Another important observation which needs mention here is that the current back-log of unemployment at around 9 per cent equivalent to 35 million persons is too high and every effort needs to be made not only to arrest the rising trend, but to actually reduce it during the Tenth Plan period itself. Similarly the mandated reduction in the poverty rate of 5 percentage points during the Tenth Plan and another 10 percentage points during the Eleventh Plan, as stipulated in the Approach Paper, will still have more than 11 per cent of the population or about 130 million people, below the poverty line in 2012. Every effort, therefore, needs to be made to reduce the poverty rate even faster.[17] These figures clearly indicate the graveness of the situation. This problem has been drawing the attention of our planners, particularly since the 1980s but the problem continues to persist.

There is growing impatience in the country at the fact that a large number of our people continued to live in abject poverty and there are alarming gaps in social attainments even after five decades of planning. There must, therefore, be willingness to modify policies and institutions based on past experience. Keeping in mind the changes that have been taking place in the Indian economy and in the rest of the world.[18] There is therefore, an express need to re-define our strategies. This re-definition is necessary both at the central government level and also at the state Government level. It is now generally recognised that government in the past tended to take on too many responsibilities, imposing severe strain on its limited financial and administrative capabilities and also stifling individual initiative. An all pervasive government role may have been necessary at a stage where private sector capabilities were un-developed, but the situation has changed dramatically in this respect. It is clear that industrial growth in future will depend largely upon the performance of the private sector.[19] It can, therefore, be clearly seen that the Tenth plan argues new strategy, a paradigm shift so far as above growth and development policy is concerned. Inspite of the shift in focus about the role of the State in development the Tenth Plan argued for agricultural sector primacy in the strategy for the Plan. It clearly stated that agricultural development must be viewed as a core element of the Plan, since growth in the sector is likely to lead to the widest spread of benefits specially to the rural poor. The first generation of reforms concentrated on the industrial economy and reforms in the agricultural sector were neglected. This must change in the Tenth Plan.[20] It was argued that the growth strategy of the Tenth Plan must ensure rapid growth of those sectors which are most likely to create gainful employment opportunities and deal with the policy constraints which discourage growth of employment.[21] There was, thus concerns expressed in Plan Document about the generating of employment opportunities to address the issue of poverty in a sense.

The Tenth Plan further observed that the policy approach to agriculture particularly in the 1990 has been to secure increased production to subsidiaries in inputs such as power, water and fertilizer, rather than through building new capital assets in irrigation, power and rural infrastructure. This strategy has run into serious difficulties. The Plan therefore, argued for a new approach to agricultural policy, based on careful assessment of current constraints and possibilities.[22] This new approach was supposed to be based on the earlier experience in this sector. We have thus seen the steps initiated during the Ninth and Tenth Plan period for India's response to new economic policy. We tried to look into the objectives, strategies and initiatives adopted by the planners to achieve growth, to generate employment and ultimately eradicate poverty. How far these plan initiatives have yielded results is a matter of analysis and debate. Let us now go into the analysis and assess as to how far the paradigm shift has helped the general mass of our people, particularly the rural poor, living below the poverty line. This analysis will be in a broader context as well as in the context of the selected States. We shall base over analysis on the data and information gathered through various sources during the course of our study.

IMPACT ANALYSIS

No fruitful purpose will be served unless we are able to objectively analyze the impact of the various policy initiatives taken for economic reforms in the post-90 scenario. Our limited focus will be on the population which is categorised as 'poor' with regard to their economic status alongwith other sectoral reforms introduced for the purposes of achieving growth.

Sometimes back it was reported by the UNDP that it will take India until 2016 to catch up with high income countries.[23] The Human Development Report makes a disturbing observation on widening disparities between and within rich and poor countries. Twenty years ago, a person born in sub-Sahara Africa would expect to live 24 years less than his counter part in a rich country. Today that gap is 33 years. World trade has increased, but OSED countries still account for two third of all exports. That growing inequality is part of India's reform story is an established fact.[24] The fruits of world trade have been redistributed within the poorer countries, with no significant transfer happening from the rich to the poor. The OECD remains the biggest anti-globaliser, persisting with trade barriers in agriculture and commodities. In

India's case accretion of capital has not been accompanied by improved living standards for all. In its chasm between growth and welfare'. India is a unique case. Country that have had a comparable growth trajectory over the last few decades, such as Brazil, are at least 50 place ahead of us in the HDR in the seas. We laud our success as democracy, but this contradiction is an appaling failure. A democracy that offers civic liberties but can not ensure physical survival in a country that is not poor anymore, is a curious thing indeed. However, it appears that our political class is waking up to shame of death and disease.[25] There is still the dilemma of growth with justice and growth without justice.

Conversely, it is argued that the Indian economy has gathered considerable strength in the last 10 years. It has become the fourth or fifth largest economy in the world. It was the eighth fastest growing economy in the world during the year 1980-1998. The following table provides the trends of some major macro economic indicators from 1991 to 2002.

A look at the table above makes it clear that the economy picked up after 1991 – 92. Our growth rate has been higher than many countries of the world. There have been substantial foreign fund inflows. The FDI inflows have also gone up to about 4 billion US dollars in 2001-02. One tends to argue that during this period the economy showed healthy signs of growth. There are some negative symptom as well. On the negative side we have some black areas. The Indian polity has not stabilised. The coalition government always has swords hanging over their heads. Managing coalition conflicts has become a more urgent task for political leadership than managing the nation and its economy. Political and social fragmentations have increased. Corruption has gone up and become more

Table 4.2

SOME KEY INDICATORS OF THE INDIAN ECONOMY (1991-2002)

Sl. No.	*Item*	*1990-91*	*1991-92*	*1998-99*	*1999-2000*	*2001-01*	*2001-02*
1.	GDP Growth Rate (at constant factor cost)%	56	1.3	6.5	6.1	4.0	5.4
2.	Gross Domestic Investment/GDP (%)	26.3	22.6	22.7	24.3	24.0	NA
3.	Gross Domestic Saving/GDP (%)	23.1	22.0	21.7	23.2	23.4	23.6
4.	Inflation rate MPI (%)	12.1	13.6	5.9	3.3	7.1	4.4
5.	Gross Fiscal Deficit (as % of GDP)	6.6	4.7	5.1	5.4	5.5	5.7
6.	Internal Market Borrowing (as % of GDP)	12.4	NA	16.4	18.4	20.7	22.0
7.	Total External Debt (as % of GDP)	28.7	38.7	24.3	23.6	22.2	NA
8.	FDI net inflows (as % of GDP)	0.03	0.05 (app)	.0.6	0.5	0.4	0.6 (app)
9.	Gross NPAs of Public Sector Banks (Crore Rs.)	-	-	57.710	53.033	59.773	NA
10.	Central Govt. Expenditure (as % of GDP)	17.3	16.2	14.7	15.4	15.3	16.4
11.	Central Govt. Receipts (as % of GDP)	15.3	15.2	14.7	15.4	15.3	16.4
12.	Foreign Exchange Reserves (billion US dollars)	5.8	9.2	32.5	38.0	42.3	51.06

Source: Economic Survey, Govt. of India (2001-2002)

Note:

(a) Some figures pertaining to the years 2000-01 and 2001-02 are provisional or based on advance estimates.

(b) NPAs (Non-Performing Assets)

widespread.[26] These are some of the negatives which one can identify inspite of the show of growth that the economy has promised.

It might be worth noting here the United Nation's World Summit focussed attention on the plight of poor countries. To reduce poverty should these countries focus on faster growth or on reducing economic disparities? Is economic growth faster with high or low inequality? The World Bank 2006 *World Development Report*, 'Equality and Development', makes the case that this commonly asked question is misguided. In the long-term, efficiency and equality are complements not substitutes.[27] Equity is not same as equality. By equity we mean equality of opportunities, where opportunities are the factors that make it possible for people to generate certain income and achieve a certain level of well being. In an equitable society, all have the same opportunities to pursue a life of their choosing, whether this in terms of acquiring an education, obtaining credit, finding a job or participating in the public debates, regardless of their country of birth, the wealth and social status of their parents, or their gender, race, caste, ethnicity or social class.[28] The distribution of income, education levels, wealth and other assets will typically be unequal in an equitable society, because people differ in their effort they make, in their desire to bear risks, are in the way they process information. Such inequality of incomes is not only acceptable, but often desirable for the incentives it provides. What is not acceptable is inequality that desires from lack of opportunities and discrimination. Citizens of developed countries live on average about 20 years longer, get at least six more years of schooling and have better health and choose from a wide range of option to fulfil their potential than their peers in low-income countries. While there is no systematic relationship between income inequality and growth, in the *World Development Report* 2006 we argue that equity and growth are in the long run complementary.[29]

There are two main reasons why equity is good for growth. First, lack of opportunities have initiative and deprives societies of the talent and effort of some of the member. Second, equity is good for growth because societies with an equitable distribution of resources tend to have more equitable political arrangements, where a majority of the citizen, and not just an elite, participate directly and indirectly in public decision making. If equity is such a good thing, then why are many societies deeply inequitable? Societies that start off with an inequitable distribution of resources tend to put in place inequitable economic and political institution. So inequity is perpetuated across generation, because elite control power and capture the benefits from economic activities. This is not only unjust, it is economically inefficient. Elite that capture power to their own benefit prevent large parts of the population from realising their economic potential.[30] While history is important in determining equity, change is possible. Indeed, history is full of good for both equity and efficiency are available, or in response to political changes. Where there is a political base for action, many policies and programmes can extend opportunities to the poor, but expanding equity so as to faster growth can also require actions that limit elite capture. Opening up the financial system, reducing the concentration or market power in certain sectors, controlling the negative consequences of corporatism, ensuring transparency and accountability of government action at the central, and local level and so on. These recommendations apply to poor and rich countries alike, but rich countries have the additional responsibility to support reform of global markets to stop discrimination against poor countries, and reform of global governance to give them greater voice and participation.[31] We have tried to enter into this debate of equity and development to see the concern it expresses about the majority of the population whose problem still need rational attention from the policy as well as the programme promulgation.

THE SCENARIO IN THE SELECTED AREAS

We have tried to provide an impact analysis after the paradigm shift at the national level. Let us now focus our attention in the selected areas of our study i.e. the States of U.P. and Karnataka. We would like to see the scenario after the globalisation and liberalisation with reference to rural development particularly the situation concerning the rural poor. In order, therefore, to formulate our opinion we have based our observation on both types of data which includes the primary as well as the secondary sources. We have so far based our observation on the data collected through the secondary sources during the course of our study. We now propose to briefly analyse the development scenario after the introduction of policy of liberalisation on the basis of primary sources. We collected information on this aspect from the officials as well as non-officials through a structured schedule (copy enclosed as Annexure I). We shall now try to look into the opinion expressed by these sections on various questions put to them during our field investigation. The main objective was to elicit their opinion on the impact of paradigm shift on the development scenario in the country in general and their own areas of operation in particular. The detailed tables have been annexed as Annexure II, here we present the analysis on the selected ones.

It is heartening to note that majority of the respondents were quite aware of the shift that has taken place in the development sector. They were asked to react to the question as to whether they are aware of paradigm shift in India's development focus. Majority of the respondents who were officials at the district level (78%) opined in favour of the question (Table – 26). Only about 22 per cent of the officials were not quite aware of the paradigm shift that has taken place in the development of the country. Almost similar question was put to non-officials as well to know their reaction. They were asked to give their opinion on the question as to how far they feel the new paradigm has helped economic growth. It is interesting to note that about 47% of the respondents in the non-officials category felt 'not at all' and about 40% reported 'to some extent'. This opinion does not go well with the opinion expressed by the officials of the same region. It signifies the difference in perception of the issues of paradigm shift. The perception of the non-officials on the impact of paradigm shift seems to be quite different from the perception of the officials who are supposed to be responsible for effecting the paradigm shift in the field.

In the post-economic reform scenario, we wanted to ascertain from the respondents their perception about the role of the State. In view of this, the respondents (non-officials) were asked to give their opinion as to how far they feel that the role of State in development has reduced. It is interesting to note that about 67 per cent of the respondents (Table – 29) opined that the role of the State in development has not reduced 'at all'. Only about one-fourth of these were of the opinion that the role of the State has been reduced 'to some extent'. Almost similar question was addressed to the officials. We asked them whether they see any policy change in the development process during the post-90, period. Almost 67 per cent of the respondents opined in favour while we have one-third of the respondents who did not agree. Here again, therefore, there appears a clear cut difference in perception about the issue.

In order to assess the impact of liberalisation, we wanted to know the reaction of the officials as well as non-officials who have been associated with the development process in their respective regions. The officials were asked as to how far they agree that post-90, development has helped India's socio-economic development. In response to this query the officials were divided. Almost one-third of the respondents opined that it has 'not at all' helped the socio-economic development. The rest of the respondents agreed to the question and they differed only in the degree of help. (Table – 28 – Officials).

Subsequently, we asked the non-official respondents as to how far the new paradigm has helped the different sectors. Their response is presented in the Table - 30 Non-Official.

It can be seen from the figures given in the table above that there is a clear indication that this shift in the paradigm has not helped at all with regard to the sector mentioned therein. One can identify the infrastructure as the only sector wherein the respondents felt that it has helped 'to some extent', otherwise, in all other sectors, majority of the respondents have opined that it has not helped at all. It is, therefore, a matter which needs serious attention of the policy planners as we see little impact of the enormous investment which is being provided in different sectors without much visible impact.

There is an impression that the economic reforms have generally been beneficial to the corporate sector in comparison to other social sectors. We, thus, wanted to ascertain the validity of this general perception about economic reforms. The respondents (officials) were asked to give their opinion as to how far the paradigm shift has helped the corporate sector. The responses received, by and large, confirm the general perception that the economic reforms have benefited the corporate sector. Only about 4 per cent of the respondents opined 'not at all' (Table – 29 – Officials). The non-officials too felt that this is going to help the corporate sector. Majority of the respondents (80 per cent - Table – 35 – Non-Officials) felt the same way.

On the contrary we wanted to know as to whether the economic reforms have helped the dis-advantaged sections of the society. The non-officials were asked to give their opinion as to how far the new paradigm will help the disadvantage sections of the society. The majority of the respondents (60 per cent) expressed the opinion that it will help 'not at all'. This is in conformity with the answers given by the respondents in the officials category as well wherein they had expressed that it will help the corporate sector. Further, in a supplementary query, the non-officials were asked to give their opinion as to how far they think the new paradigm will help out the market-forces. In response to this question more than half (53 per cent – Table – 32 – Non-officials) respondents opined that the new paradigm will help out the market-forces. The initial fears which were shown by some sections, tends to be supplemented by the opinion expressed by the respondents, particularly, the non-officials.

We earlier noted the opinion expressed by the non-officials about various sectors. Let us now take note of the opinion expressed by the officials regarding various sectors of the economy. In this connection we asked the officials as to how far they think the paradigm shift has helped the agricultural sector. The officials seem to feel that it has helped the agricultural sector as only 11 per cent (Table-30 – Officials) opined 'not at all', which mean that the rest of the respondents agreed that it has helped, only variation in the response was about the degree of help. The officials over-whelmingly (78 per cent – Table-31 – Officials) felt that the paradigm shift has helped the industrial sector 'to some extent' and about 11 per cent expressed 'to a large extent' response category. It can, therefore, be seen that except a marginal percentage of respondents, all of them felt that the paradigm shift has helped the industrial sector.

In order to assess the impact of paradigm shift on the urban middle class, which is otherwise considered a struggling class, we wanted to know the opinion of the officials who themselves may be constituting the urban middle class group. It may be interesting to note that more than half (55.56 per cent – Table-32 – Officials) expressed that the paradigm shift has only 'to some extent' helped the urban middle class. In this context it may be noted that about one fourth (22 per cent) respondents were of the opinion that the urban middle class has 'not at all' benefited. This percentage may be small, but it does represent a class of people who feel that urban middle class continues to struggle inspite of the paradigm shift. This in brief is the assessment of the impact of the paradigm shift in India's development with reference to the selected areas.

One would like to make a reference here of the coverage brought about by the *India Today*[32] about the best and the worst States in India. This assessment has been on the performance of the States taking into account eight factors *viz.*: agriculture, industrial environment, consumer market, health, education, law and order, infrastructure and budget and prosperity. All these factors are concerned with development and the equality of life of people living in these States. Our anxiety was to know about our selected States as to how they stand in the assessment done by the leading news channel of the country. Under this survey the States of Uttar Pradesh is at number 17 out of the 20 States amongst the reported States whereas Karnataka stands at number eight. It may also be noted that both these States did not register any change in their performance change on the factors noted above between 2004 to 2005 period. It can be seen in the cover story that Karnataka is placed slightly higher than Uttar Pradesh in various factors mentioned above. The problem of regional imbalance has also come out rather clearly in the aforesaid survey.

We, therefore, find a mixed response to the concept of paradigm shift in India's development. The change is perceived in several sectors which have registered growth. At the same time reported death of farmers in both the selected States raises a number of questions about the feasibility of the new paradigm. There seems little respite for the small farmer. This re-inforces the role of the State in the development process. The debate seems to be still on.

After having analysed the scenario in the selected areas, we would like to briefly discuss the approach of the Eleventh Five-Year Plan in the context of the issues raised earlier. It is worthwhile to note that the Eleventh Plan allegedly provides an opportunity to restructure policies to achieve a new vision of growth that will be much more broad based and inclusive, bringing about a faster reduction in poverty and helping bridge the divides that are currently the focus of so much attention.

Rapid growth is an essential part of our strategy for two reasons. Firstly, it is only in a rapidly growing economy that we can expect to sufficiently raise the incomes of the mass of our population to bring about a general improvement in living condition. Secondly, rapid growth is necessary to generate the resources needed to provide basic services to all. Work done within the Planning Commission and elsewhere suggests that the economy can accelerate from 8 per cent per year to an average of around 9 per cent over the Eleventh Plan period, provided appropriate policies are put in place. With population growing at 1.5 per cent per year, 9 per cent growth in GDP would double the real per capita income in 10 years. This must be combined with policies that will ensure that this per capita income growth is broad based, benefiting all sections of the population, specially those who have thus far remained deprived.[33] It could be seen as an effort towards addressing the issues which we have noted earlier.

The Eleventh Plan further provides that the key elements of the strategy for inclusive growth must be an all out effort to provide the mass of our people the access to basic facilities, such as health, education, clean drinking water, etc. While in the short run they determine economic opportunities for the future. It is important to recognize that access to these basic services is not necessarily assured simply by a rise in per capita income. Government at different levels have to ensure the provision of these basic services and this must be an essential part of strategy for the inclusive growth. At the same time it is important to recognize that better health and education are the necessary pre-condition for sustained long-term growth.[34] It may be noted that in order to provide the basic necessities to rural India, the Minimum Needs Programme was launched long back. But this could not achieve the desired goal. Again, decades after that effort the Eleventh Plan feels the necessity of that strategy for long-term growth.

While encouraging private sector growth, the Eleventh Plan would also ensure a substantial increase in the allocation of public resources for Plan programme in critical areas. This will support the growth strategy and ensure inclusiveness. These resources will be easier to mobilise if the economy grows rapidly. A new stimulus to public sector investment in particularly important in agriculture and infrastructure and both the Centre and the States have to take steps to mobilize resources to make this possible. The growth component of this strategy is, therefore, important for two reasons: a) it will contribute directly by raising income levels and employment b) it will help finance programmes that will ensure more brand broad and inclusive growth.[35] It may be noted here that the country had experimented with the growth model in the initial years of our planned development. But that suffered from several inadequacies which were realised and subsequently change in strategy could be seen in later models of development.

The economic reforms were expected to address issues facing the third world counties. As a result of economic reforms implemented by successive governments over the past decades and a half, our economy has matured in several important aspects. It is now much more integrated with the world economy and has benefited from this integration in many ways. One of the benefit derived from global integration is the increased inflow of foreign direct investment (FDI). FDI increased from an average of $3.7 billion in the Ninth Plan period to average $5.7 billion in the first four years of the Tenth Plan. The National Common Minimum Programme states that the country needs and can absorb three times the amount of FDI that it gets. This is a reasonable target and can be achieved in the Eleventh Plan.[36] The target thus set forth, is achieved or not only time will tell.

The planned effort has also not been able to achieve success in regional development sector. It has been expressed that the regional backwardness is another important issue for our planned effort. Differences across States have always been a cause of concern but there exists imbalances within the States as well. Backward districts of otherwise well performing States, present a dismal picture of intra-State independence and neglect. The Centre and the States will together have to deal with this problem on a priority basis otherwise discontent, injustice did frustration will only breed extremism.[37] We have noted this problem in the earlier pages of the book during various phases of planned development. The Eleventh Plan has again focused on the urgency of the issue.

These are in brief the areas being addressed by the approach of the Eleventh Five-Year Plan. It could be observed here that the Plan realistically tries to look at the problem facing the country in terms of growth and plans as to counter the problem faced in the growth process.

REFERENCES

1. *Towards a New Paradigm in Sustainable Rural Development*, Andrew Shephered, Palgrave, New York, 2001, p. 17.
2. Eighth Five-Year Plan, Planning Commission, Government of India, New Delhi (preface to the plan).
3. *Ibid.*, p. 2.
4. *Ibid.*
5. *Poverty Curtain: Choices for the Third World*, Mahbub-ul-Haque, 1985.
6. Ninth Five-Year Plan, Planning Commission, Govt. of India, New Delhi, p. 1.1.
7. *Ibid.* p. 1.2.

8. *Ibid.*
9. *Ibid.*
10. *Ibid.*
11. *Ibid.*
12. Ibid, p.1.8.
13. Tenth Five-Year Plan, Planning Commission, Govt. of India, New Delhi, p. 1.
14. *Ibid.* p. 4.
15. *Ibid.*
16. *Ibid.* pp. 5-6.
17. *Ibid.* p. 7.
18. *Ibid.*
19. *Ibid.*
20. Ibid, p. 9 (box 1.3)
21. *Ibid.*
22. *Ibid.* p. 14.
23. UNDP Human Development Report, 2005.
24. *Times of India,* Lucknow, Sept. 9, 2005, (editorial).
25. *Ibid.*
26. *India's Reform Imperatives* (Retrospect and Prospects), ed. By T.N. Dhar, IIPA, U.P. Regional Branch, Lucknow, 2003, p. 40.
27. All That You Can't Leave Behind, Growth Bandawagan Can not Afford to Exclude the Poor by Frangois Bourguiguon and Shantayanan Devranajn, Times of India, Lucknow, September 24, 2005.
28. *Ibid.*
29. *Ibid.*
30. *Ibid.*

31. *Ibid.*

32. *India Today*, August 15, 2005.

33. Towards Faster and More Inclusive Growth–An Approach to the 11th Five-Year Plan (2007-2012), Planning Commission, Government of India, New Delhi, 2006, pp. 1-2.

34. *Ibid.* p. 2.

35. *Ibid.* p. 3.

36. *Ibid.* p. 5.

37. *Ibid.* p. 10.

Chapter 5

Problem Areas

Several paradigms have been experimented during the five decades of planned development in India. We have already analysed various aspects of these development paradigms in the chapters earlier. It is now proposed to highlight some of the important problems and concerns during the post-90's development period which has witnessed the paradigm shift. Various aspects of the problem like the social, economic, political and administrative are proposed to be addressed in this part of the book. It may be noted that development per se continues to be a multi disciplinary concept and therefore, there are several aspects which affect and influence the policy and programme formulation as well as implementation. These aspects have their own impact on the development ethos, hence in the following pages an attempt is being made to address these problems for a better understanding of the issues involved.

In the early fifties the country was faced with several problems which it tried to address from the very beginning. One of the major problems that the country has been facing was concerned with poverty and unemployment of vast majority of our population particularly living in the rural areas. The concern shown by successive Governments is reflected in the planning exercises done during the five decades of planned development. It, however, continues to be a serious concern even after the paradigm shift was introduced in the country. The information collected from the selected States has shown that there is little change so far as this sector is concerned. The suicidal deaths reported in several States of India, developed or not so developed, puts a question mark on the very premise of development and growth. What purpose it is going to serve if the farmers continued to lead a life of abject poverty and are forced to commit suicide.

It is being argued that growth bandwagon can not afford to exclude the poor. We have, in the earlier chapter noted the World Bank's, 2006 *World Development Report*, 'Equity and Development'. It makes a case that this commonly asked question is misguided. In the long-term, efficiency and equity are complements not substitutes. This may be logically tenable, but it can not be denied that poverty manifests itself in various ways. The case of India is peculiarly different from other third world countries. Its long historical traditions at times function as barriers in the over all societal processes. The question of poverty is not only confined to economic, but it manifests itself, in several other ways which hampers the development and quality of life of people who constitute the poor.

India being an ancient nation has several socio-cultural traditions which are deep rooted in its social fabric. These traditions and values often contradict the values associated with equity and freedom. There has been a school of thought earlier which highlighted the non-economic factors in economic development and these can safely be construed to be the social factors. These social factors have continuously been influencing the developmental process across the country. The failure of our development effort may be because of several other factors, but social factors do constitute the core factor in explaining the failure of our development effort. Lack of appreciation of the importance of their role in the overall development, often lead to lack of achievement of the desired objectives.

The attitude of different classes and castes of people about the social issues, norms and values plays an important role in the formulation as well as implementation of development policies and programmes since the Indian social order has remained a fragmented social order, its diversity sometimes is seen as a weakness rather than a strength. Different caste groups many a times tend to benefit their own caste people which affect the general cause. In eradicating poverty, the effort should be to tackle the root causes which perpetuate poverty. These could be possible if we give a serious thought to these social issues and values which would help solve the problem and not perpetuate them. This is not to suggest that the people in concerned circles are not aware of them, we are only trying to provide an added focus to their importance. We feel if these social issues are addressed in a right perspective many of the problems could be minimised.

There appears to be a lack of appreciation about the problem, particularly faced by the unprivileged and the under privileged sections of our society. Looking at the status of education, health, infant mortality and other indicators, we find that those who are at helm of affairs to manage these sectors seem to have little empathy. For the last several decades the amount of expenditure that has gone into these sectors, is difficult to comprehend but the level of improvement is there for any one to see. When a death due to hunger is reported, the official machinery immediately denies and puts different claims. These are deaths owing to diseases, malnutrition, hunger, but the official machinery, instead of removing the cause for such incidents, questions the reliability of the news report. There seems to be a sheer lack of appreciation of the problem faced by the poor which need to be rationally addressed.

The economic development has been consistently facing problem in terms of a suitable development model. During the last five decades of development we have experimented with several models but problems continued to influence the achievement levels. The problems have been in reducing the gap between the rich and the poor, removing poverty, increasing opportunities for employment, increasing agricultural and industrial production, rationalisation of distribution system, infrastructural development, so on and so forth. All these are linked with proper economic development which can address towards these. Taking a broader perspective of the country as whole, we find that the gap between the rich has not decreased but if the official figures are to be believed, it has increased. The rich have become richer and the poor have become poorer. This is a problem which has to be tackled sooner than later.

Amongst the selected States, the economic status of Uttar Pradesh can be termed as serious. During the post-reform period of 1993-94 to 2000-2001, the real GSDP at factor cost (1993-94) in divided Uttar Pradesh had an average annual growth of 4.22 per cent as against all-India average growth of 6.3 per cent. During the most recent period of 2001-02 to 2002-2003, the average growth has been just about 2.24 per cent as against all-India average of 4.88 per cent. The result of poor overall economic activity and high population growth is reflected in extremely slow growth in per capita income as compared to all-India growth figures. During 2002-2003 Uttar Pradesh had a per capita real income that was 47.7 per cent less than the all-India average. This is a considerable deterioration from 1980-81, when it had 17.2 per cent less than the all-India average. People are migrating from Uttar Pradesh because of the income gap between Uttar Pradesh and rest of India.[1]

It may be noted here that Uttar Pradesh has seen a fall in the incidence of poverty from 41 per cent in 1993-94 to 31 per cent in 1999-2000. However, this achievement is far below the all-India figures of 26 per cent. The difference in poverty level with respect to national figures are more pronounced in urban areas compared to the rural areas. Rural poverty has gone down by 11 percentage points as against a fall of 4 percentage points in urban Uttar Pradesh. At sub-regional level, approximately 44 per cent of total poor people in divided Uttar Pradesh during 199-2000 lived in eastern part of the State. The corresponding figures for Western, Central and Bundelkhand were 28, 24 and 4 per cent respectively.[2] These figures themselves reveal the poverty scenario in this State. But an alarming fact is that people have been committing suicide because of various reasons. The state of the economy, therefore, is such which needs serious attention from the powers that be.

There are several weaknesses and threats to the progress of Uttar Pradesh. Although Uttar Pradesh can claim to be the largest producer of food-grains in the country, the yield and per capita production is much lower than other foodgrain producers in the country, particularly, Punjab and Haryana. Foodgrain yield in Uttar Pradesh is almost half that of Punjab. Low per capita income creates a vicious circle, which needs to be broken through government intervention.[3] Interestingly the government interested in rural sector after the Reforms has been on a low priority. The farmers have been taking loans to meet the expenditure on agricultural production. The production on the one hand has been low and on the other dependency on monsoon further increases their problem. In order to address to these problems, alternative sources of income need to be generated.

Clearly, capital in Uttar Pradesh is not as productive as it is elsewhere, while the State displays average level of industrialisation. Analysis of three-digit level ASI data also indicates that Uttar Pradesh is far behind from the leaders in production share in each of its 22 major manufacturing sectors, which contribute more than 80 per cent of manufactured output. The gross value added (GVA) from top five three-digit industries of India is of the order of 41.89 per cent, in which the share of Uttar Pradesh is just 1.8 per cent.[4]

The most important threat to the States' economy comes from the financial management of the State government. As on March 31, 2003 Uttar Pradesh had a liability including revenues and deposits, of the order of Rs. 103117.5 crores, which had increased to Rs. 119870.09 crore on March 31, 2004 (an increase of 163 per cent). It is estimated that the debt (net of revenues and deposits) would have gone up to 44.5 per cent of 45 DP by March 31, 2005. As against this, the average debt in 15 major States such as Andhra Pradesh, Karnataka, Tamil Nadu, Maharashtra, and Gujrat having debts of the over of 28.85, 25.12, 26.84, 25.58 and 33.93 per cent of GSDP respectively.[5] Uttar Pradesh pays about 29 per cent (average of 2000-03) of its revenue receipt as interest on debt and at the same time maintaining a persistent primary deficit of more than 1.0 per cent of GSDP. This makes debt situation in Uttar

Pradesh unsustainable.[6] This state of economy can hardly be termed encouraging and also explains the problem that the State has been facing in the contemporary scenario.

It is not only the problem of backward States like Uttar Pradesh, the developed States too have been facing problem in respect to the question of right choice for economic development. This is being raised here because there are suicidal deaths of farmers reported not only in backward States, but also developed States like Punjab and Karnataka. There is therefore, a continuous need for review of the strategies of development in order to have proper economic development where equity and development could supplement each other.

There is no denying the fact that political ideologies and affiliation also affect the development ethos. In a democratic polity the political process influences the development process in more than one ways. We have, therefore, to understand and analyse these political concerns to address the issues concerned with development. At the macro as well as the micro level, the political outfits both, help and hamper the development of the area depending upon their own political leanings. We have been continuously observing the impact of political rivalry in development policy and programmes. Even if we do not go into the history of such incidents, the current scenario across the country will provide us sufficient information to support this conviction. For example, in Uttar Pradesh, the government is headed by Samajwadi Party where as at the Centre we have a coalition led by the Congress Party. Many a times matters have been reported about the Central funding of a project being denied or not considered by the State Government as it may give some political mileage to the Congress Party. Further, whosoever, becomes the Chief Minister, tries to overdo the things for their home constituency whereas the general cause may suffer. There has been criticism by many political parties of the investments being made in the constituency of the Chief Minister. However, there are counter arguments too in support of such investments. It is argued that it is the privilege of the chief minister to nourish the constituency and there is nothing politically wrong in this.

Apart from these particular wishes and instances, there have been problems in approaching a problem and the issues concerning development. During the last five decades of our planned development several programmes were initiated by one political party but they were either stopped or modified by other political parties when they came to power. The recent examples can be found after reforms were introduced in the country. During the coalition led by Bhartiya Janta Party, there was a clear-cut policy about disinvestment. So long as this coalition was in power, disinvestment was an accepted policy option of the government. But after the fall of BJP – led coalition in the general elections, that followed the new coalition government led by the Congress Party revised the policy regarding the disinvestment apart from many more other policy issues. The role of the Left parties has been quite crucial in the governance as they were supporting the alliance and are a force to reckon with. This, therefore, had a telling impact on the new UPA Coalition government where the concerns of development are seen differently.

It is also to be noted that development across the world has encouraged investment of a very high magnitude. India too has witnessed the investment gallore for the last five decades or so. The quantum of investment in the development sector somehow or the other did not match the result it was expected of such investments. On the contrary, it has been a story of corruption spreading through different levels of political and administrative organisation. It reached to such a high proportion that once Mr. Rajiv Gandhi, the then Prime Minister of India made an observation that only 15 paise of a rupee reaches the targetted group and the rest 85 paise goes elsewhere. We can now see that there is no dearth of cases, some reported and the rest unreported, about political corruption in the country. One can find 'n' number of people having income and assets much beyond their known source of income. This, therefore, is one of the explanations for the failure or the lack of achievement in our development effort. It has now reached a stage of cancer which is eating away the very vitals of limited resources.

There have been committees and commissions appointed by the Government of India to look into this aspect of our governance. There are a number of institutions to check corruption by public officials. But there seems to be little respite as people in high offices often compromise on values and virtues of ethics. So long as therefore, this malaise of corruption is not checked, the fruits of development will hardly reach the targetted groups. The quality of life of people will continue to suffer unless this is effectively addressed by the concerned circles. The political process as well as the development process has to be corruption free in order to get the desired results.

Apart from the political problem, administrative problems too occupy an important place in any discussion about the problem facing development. Some space is, therefore, needed to briefly highlight those which have been hampering the development in the sense that benefit have not been reaching to the target groups.

We can see that administrative problems are associated with the structure, functions, the financial management, supervision and control, values and attitudes, administrative corruption to list a few. The democratic polity and colonial administrative structure, this is how we started after independence. This, though provided the much-needed continuity then so far as the administrative process was concerned, it also left the gaps which could not be bridged even after the system has been through for more than five decades. These gaps have been visible at the district level, the cut off level of Indian administration. For the purposes of development, new organisations like Community Development Blocks and National Extension Service Blocks were created, but the traditional district administration kept its hold on the district for almost all-important purposes. Not only the regulatory administration, but the development administration too remained for a larger period with the Collector of the district. It has been realised that the type of administration needed different kind of approaches and orientation to address the issues created with these types of adminis-tration. In the absence of this differentiation, the development administration perhaps could not achieve which was formally required of it. Development adminis-tration perhaps needs a different set of approaches, planning, strategy, training and orientation than regulatory administration. This has been one of the major problems of the district level particularly.

The administrative problems seem to be continuing even after the introduction of economic reforms in the country. There has been little change in the administrative system which we inherited from the British. The major elements of secrecy, rigidity, redtapism and its generalist orientation have continued to persist in the Indian administration. The post-reform administration needs openness, flexibility, speedy delivery system, transparency and information sharing. This has somehow not been there in the administrative system which has created problems for rapid economic development during the post reform period. In the State like Uttar Pradesh, the administration has almost failed to respond to the new demands. Consequently, we find that the State has further gone down so far as the progress and development scenario is concerned.

It is not only the so-called traditional administrative structure, that has been problematic in efficient development administration but there has been attitudinal problem as well in bureaucratic performance. The manner in which the poverty eradication programmes have been implemented over the years and across the country shows the extent of sensitivity of the administration towards poor. Majority of funds have allegedly been not properly utilised for the purpose it was meant. On the one hand the investment in the sector kept increasing and on the other, the gap between the rich and the poor kept rising. There has hardly been any respite for the large population living below the poverty line. The paradigm shift seems to have further aggravated the miseries of such population. The reason for this could be in the very premise of policy shift. It seems to be more inclined towards liberalisation, competition, openness, transparency to boost business and commerce rather than address to the problems of poverty, hunger, regional imbalance and the likes. This gets reflected in the performance chart of the government.

The concern of new economic policy could be well revived provided it adequately addresses the concerns of the disadvantaged and the poorer sections of the society.

The purpose will not be served if the new economic policy caters to the corporate sector and leaves the rest to the vagaries of the market forces. Under no circumstances should the poor be left unattended and uncared for. The State and the administration are duty bound to provide every class of people a dignified life, to all its citizen. These economic reforms, therefore, necessitate an administrative reform in order to facilitate the achievements commensurate with goals and objectives. The goals of liberalised economy can hardly be adequately achieved through a rigid, dogmatic and red-tapist administrative system. This will continue to create problems unless addresses through rationalistic reform measures.

In the list of administrative problems, one can highlight another important problem of the misuse of authority by people occupying such positions. There have been cases and some of them have been reported and action taken, about the use of public office for personal gains. This has led to corruption in the administrative system. There has been an official machinery in existence to check and prevent corruption in public offices. But these rules and regulations and the machinery has not been able to cut much ice and this has become a deep-rooted malaise. This is a serious problem facing our administrative system and has surely hampered the development process. Some has been arguing that corruption has not been institutionalised. This cannot be considered a healthy sign for any system to function and grow. This has to be seriously addressed by all concerned before it is too late.

These are some of the problems which we have tried to indicate. This is only a tip of the ice-berg. India is a huge country and therefore, a small problem takes huge proportion. A similar huge effort is needed to counter these problems.

REFERENCES

1. Uttar Pradesh Development Report, Planning Commission, Government of India, New Delhi, Vol. I, 2007, p. 37.
2. *Ibid.* pp. 37-38.
3. *Ibid.* p. 38.
4. *Ibid.* p. 39.
5. *Ibid.* p. 39.
6. *Ibid.*

Chapter 6

Summary and Conclusion

The term development has generated considerable debate in the contemporary social science arena. The debate covers areas such as the concept, the approaches, models, strategies for societies which have achieved different development levels. There is, however, already considerable literature on the theme of development which also leads to confusion. The literature shows the concern of both the worlds, developed as well as developing. Social scientists of both the worlds have contributed their bit in the debate about development. The concept of development, however, eludes any simple or single acceptable definition. We have therefore, various connotations attached to development. It might be pertinent to briefly touch upon them before taking the discussion further.

One line of argument explains that the concept is fundamentally biological. While a concept of development may be used in respect to physical system and while it may refer also to system of ideas, the term has been most commonly associated with the organisation of living structure and life processes. Students of animal and human growth and behaviour who attempt to fit the developmental phenomena they observe into systamic relationship with other data, have frequently had recourse in one or another to the level of organisation doctrine. Not only do the biologist and the students of behaviour development have difficulty fitting phenomenon of growth or development into physical concepts, but they have a fundamental difficulty with the symbolic system into which their concept and constructs must be cast. The empirical scientist frequently distrusts the deduction approach. Certainly the empirical approach in science is still vigorous. The goal of scientific movement is to understand man and his universe. These goals must always be kept in view so that we do not mistake means for ends. The concept of development has reference to Ontogeny too. Representatives of the discipline which deal with individual organism present their understanding of the term and assess its usefulness in their several fields. The word development is notoriously one with protean meaning. It is sometimes used to connote process, sometimes the product of a process.

The concept of development incorporates different discussions reflected through different indicators. An important indicator of development is per capita income, which is determined, both by the volume of production. Some of the other indicators of development are longevity of life and mortality and fertility rates. Apart from this core indicator, there are other indicators which contribute to the realisation of the central indicators, such as the productivity of the various production activities and education, condition of housing and roads and communication. Such factors jointly contribute to pattern of living, measured to fall at different levels of development.

Today development debate has taken several sharp turns indicating radical departure from five decades. The critique of modern development theory are not restricted to alternatives, but are based on normative research for a more satisfactory and indigenous form of development, much different from dominant western paradigm. In the immediate post-war era, it was assumed that development takes place in almost all societies, expansion of industry and increased production and consumption of goods and services. By the end of 1980, the concept of sustainable development had been launched by the Brundtland Commission which defines it as "development that meets the needs of the present without compromising the ability of future generation to meet their own needs", and gave overriding priority to the essential needs of the world's poor while acknowledging the same on the environment's ability to meet present and future needs. This, in brief is the theme around which the development debate has taken shape.

Immediately after the attainment of independence the country was faced with the problem of shortage of foodgrain, lack of infrastructure in various sectors. The immediate task before the government then was to make a policy choice for future development of India. It may be noted that the creation of Planning Commission headed by the Prime Minister is one of the key steps, taken in that direction as India opted for a planned approach to development. In the context of rural India it favoured the approach called democratic decentralisation operationalised through community development and panchayati raj. These two have been the main vehicles of rural development.

India has been through five decades of planned development during which quite a few strategies, approaches and programmes were initiated to tackle the problem of development including rural development. Inspite of these efforts the problems facing the rural community did not show much improvement. Instead the gap between the rich and poor kept increasing. The decade of nineties and thereafter there is another effort through New Economic Policy. It makes a clear shift in the earlier approaches to development. Under this new paradigm, the economy was to be more liberal, open and transparent. It appeared to be consumer oriented rather than citizen-oriented. The issue therefore, to be addressed is to see as to how far this new economic policy is going to help to solve the problem of the majority of the people living in the rural India, particularly living below the poverty line. That in fact, is the acid test for this shift of the policy.

The present study briefly makes an attempt to debate the following issues:

i) To assess various strategies and models adopted for socio-economic development in the country.

ii) To examine the extent and relevance of State intervention in socio-economic development in the country.

iii) To identify the parameters for the assessment of growth and development.

iv) To examine the changes affected after the economic reforms initiated in the 90's.

v) To examine the achievement level in the process of development of the selected area.

vi) To suggest changes, if any, in the contemporary policies and strategies of development.

With the above objectives the study was undertaken. Two States, one from the north and the other from the southern region were selected namely Uttar Pradesh and Karnataka. The study made use of both the sources of data i.e. the primary as well as secondary. The primary source of data was mainly the structured schedule prepared for the purpose, for both the officials and non-officials. The secondary sources of data included official reports, files, books, reports and other published material concerned with the theme.

THE DEVELOPMENT SCENARIO

Under the development scenario we have tried to discuss various aspects of development through Five-Year Plans. Different Five-Year Plans provided for different approaches and strategies for development in the country. Looking at the first Five-Year Plan, it had a two told objective. Firstly, it aimed at correcting the dis-equilibrium in the economy caused by the war and the partition of the country. Secondly, it proposed to initiate simultaneously a process of all-round balanced development which would ensure a rising national income and a steady improvement in the living standards over a period. It provided a step in a new direction, a step which invoked greater direct responsibility for the State in providing development in all sectors of the economy and at all levels. The first plan was a first step towards the planned development.

The second plan had to carry forward the process initiated in the first Five-Year Plan period. The second plan explains its concerns and elaborates the concept of socialistic pattern of society. The second Five-Year Plan was formulated with reference to the following main objectives:

i) A sizeable increase in national income so as to raise the level of living in the country.

ii) Rapid industrialisation with particular emphasis on the development of basic and heavy industries.

iii) A large expansion of employment opportunities, and

iv) Reduction of inequalities in income and wealth and more even distribution of economic power.

The second Five-Year Plan focussed on the achievement of the objectives listed above. Increased agricultural production, improving industrial growth, developing appropriate technology for increased employment and the like were the concerns of the second plan. The first decade of development through the two Five-Year Plans centred around agriculture and industry, the two core sectors of development. The period of third Five-Year Plan represents the first stage of a decade or more of intensive development leading to a self-relient and self-growing economy. In the theme of development during the third plan the first priority becomes agriculture and added focus was attached to this sector. The second major development concerns the introduction of *Panchayati Raj*. The third aspect of community development work which was assured significance in the proposal that, along with the district, the block agency will serve as a unit of planning and development. The three Five-Year Plans implemented so far addressed specially to the problem which emerged either because of new political and economic development in the country and in the world or as a consequence of progress already achieved.

The fourth Five-Year Plan had to provide the next step forward in attaining accepted aims and objectives of Indian planning. The fourth plan aims at acceleration of the tempo of development in conditions of stability and reduced uncertainties. The fourth plan made an observation that population growth is an important variable determining the rate of improvement in per capita income. It expressed concerns over the population growth in the country.

The fifth Five-Year Plan reviewed the progress of the planned development in the country in various sectors of the economy and tried to adjust the problems faced so far in the current exercise. The fifth plan period (1975-1979) is a period when the country was faced with challenges of various kinds. The call of 'total revolution' by the JP movement created a situation which resulted in the Declaration of Emergency in the country by Mrs. Gandhi, the then Prime Minister. The general elections held after the Emergency brought Janta Party to power, replacing long rule of Congress. This also witnessed policy changes at the national level. The fifth plan did show some improvement in the growth rate. But overall, the country continued to face the problems which it was facing at the time of independence. The continuance of poverty, unemployment, lack of infrastructure and the like called for a new look towards the strategy for planned development.

It is in the light of the above that the objectives of the sixth plan were framed. The strategy adopted for the sixth plan consisted essentially of moving simultaneously to strengthening the infrastructure for both agricultural and industry so as to create condition for an acceleration in investments, output exports and to provide through special programmes designed for the purpose, increased opportunities for employment especially in the rural areas and the unorganised sector and the basic needs of the people. The sixth plan on the one hand proposed to strengthen the process of democratic decentralisation and on the other, proposed an important structural change in the form of District Rural Development Agency (DRDA) for overseeing rural development at the district level. It may be interesting to note that the entire funding for rural development was meant through the DRDA, which were also responsible for coordinating rural development with *Panchayati Raj* institution. The plan, thus, initiated certain policy changes to eradicate poverty from the rural areas.

It was asserted that the programme of development during the seventh plan, must be set against the perspectives of the next fifteen years: 1985 to 2000. In more than concrete terms this means the elimination of poverty and creating conditions of near full employment, satisfaction of basic needs of the people in terms of food, clothing and shelter, attainment of universal elementary education and access to health facility for all. The long-term strategy for the seventh plan was to take into account this objective condition in the economic and the likely development over the planning horizon. During the seventh plan period decentralisation of the planning process and full public participation in development will be pursued on the lines suggested by the working group which meant that the Collector had an increased role in the process. The development journey for four decades through seven Five-Year Plans could address only to some of the issues facing the Indian socio-economic order whereas poverty and unemployment persisted during all these years.

THE PARADIGM SHIFT

The development scenario witnessed a change in the 1990's when economic reforms were formally launched. This paradigm shift was expected to influence almost all the sectors including development of rural India. With this in view we tried to look into the impact of paradigm shift particularly the rural sector. It may be noted that the eighth Five-Year Plan was being launched at a time when the economic reforms had already been initiated. It had started to influence the public policy arena. For various plausible reasons the eighth Five-Year Plan desired to orient some of the development paradigms, since its objective is to lay a sound foundation. The ninth Five-Year Plan was launched in the 50th year of India's independence with the hope that it will take India into the new millennium. The Approach Paper to the ninth Plan accorded priority to agriculture and rural development and eradication of poverty, accelerating the growth rate of the economy with stable prices, ensuring food and nutritional security for all, particularly the vulnerable sections of the society, providing the basic minimum services of safe drinking water, primary health care facility universal primary education, shelter, connectivity to all in a time-bound manner, containing the growth rate of population, ensuring environmental sustainability of the development process through social mobilisation and participation of people at all levels are some of the priorities of the ninth Plan.

India's development strategy, like that of most of other developing countries, has evolved over successive plan periods, reflecting the growing strength of the economy, structured transformation taking place in the democratic economy and also development in the world economy. A logical argument is advanced in favour of reform to continue. The reform involves a major re-orientation of the role of the State. The Approach Paper of the tenth plan had proposed that the plan should aim at an indication target of 8% average GDP growth for the plan period. Another important observation which needs mention is that the current backlog of unemployment at around 9 per cent is high enough and needs to be made not only to invest the rising funds, but to actually reduce it during the tenth plan period itself. Similarly, the mandated reduction in the poverty rate of 5 percentage point during the tenth plan and another 10 percentage points during the eleventh plan, as stipulated in the Approach Paper will still have been more than 11 per cent of the population or about 120 million people below the poverty line in 2012.

There is growing impatience in the country at the fact that a large number of our people continued to live in object poverty and there are already gaps in social attainments even after five decades of development effort. *The Human Development Report* makes a disturbing observation on widening disparities between and within rich and poor countries. Conversely it is argued that the Indian economy has gathered considerable strength in the last 10 years. It has become the fourth or fifth largest economy in the world. The size of the economy and health trends in the economy suggest the broader achievement at the macro level. At the micro-level, the picture does not seem to be that brighter, largely looking at the conditions prevailing in rural India when the large number of farmers are forced to commit suicide for one reason or the other.

The United Nations World Summit focussed attention on the plight of the poor countries. The World Bank's 2006 *World Development Report,* 'Equity and Development', makes the case that this commonly asked question is misguided. Equity is not the same as equality. By equity we mean equality of opportunity, where opportunities are the factor that makes it possible for people to generate certain income and achieve a certain level of well being. The distribution of income, eradication levels, wealth and other assets will typically be unequal in an equitable society because people differ in the effort they make, in their desire to bear risks, or in the way they process information. There are two main reasons why equity is good for growth. Firstly, lack of opportunities harm initiatives and deprive societies of the talent and effort. Secondly, equity is good for growth because societies with an equitable distribution of resources tend to have more equitable political arrangement. This is an argument taking rounds in the post-reform period and has resulted in reduced State intervention in the development process.

There is a general impression that the Indian economy has stabilised after the paradigm shift and growth rate shows positive trends which is supplemented by the data and information collected during the course of study. Simultaneously, the data also indicates that the gap between the rich and poor has widened. It is feared that liberalisation has been beneficial more to the corporate sector than the rural sector in India. The increased growth rate has helped the economy, which can be seen in several sectors, but scenario in rural India does not match the proclamation of the government. The rural infrastructure as well as the service sector does not show the same trends. The idea of growth with justice seem to take some more time and effort.

India's development scenario has witnessed several paradigms during its long journey of planned effort. The new economic policy of liberalisation is termed as a new paradigm, and in a sense, a paradigm shift from earlier paradigm. It was expected that this will open the door for globalisation and Indian economy will be linked to the global economy for a more rapid and competitive economic development. It is more than a decade since these reforms were introduced in India. We tried to look into the areas that concerned us in the study. We have generally noted that the economy did prosper and stabilised to an extent, but it still has to address issues concerned with rural India, specially to issues concerning poverty and unemployment which continue to haunt. The progress achieved in one sector can not be fully enjoyed when the other sector is still suffering. The paradigm shift, therefore, has to effectively address these issues as they continue to pose problem for the policy planners.

Annexure – I

A STUDY OF PARADIGM SHIFT IN INDIA'S DEVELOPMENT

QUESTIONNAIRE FOR OFFICIALS

i. State:________________ ii. District:________________

iii. Block:________________ iv. Village:________________

A. GENERAL BACKGROUND

1. Name: ________________ 2. Age:________________
3. Sex: Male/Female________________
4. Present Designation (post being held):________________
5. Since when on the Position: ________________
6. Educational Qualification: ________________
7. Caste: ________________
8. Family Size – a. Adult: _______ b. Child: ______
9. Total Length of Service: ________________
10. Is wife Serving: Yes/ No ________________
11. Monthly Income – a. Family: _________ b. Individual: ______

B. DEVELOPMENT PERSPECTIVE

1. How far do you think India has developed during the last five decades?

   a. To a large extent ☐ b. To some extent ☐

   c. Not at all ☐

2. How far do you think the State should have a role in development?

   a. To a large extent ☐ b. To some extent ☐

   c. Not at all ☐

3. How far are you satisfied with the role of State in India's development?

   a. To a large extent ☐ b. To some extent ☐

   c. Not at all ☐

4. How far do you think the Government of the country has helped achieve development?

   a. To a large extent ☐ b. To some extent ☐

   c. Not at all ☐

5. How far do you think the Government at the Centre been able to eradicate poverty?

   a. To a large extent ☐ b. To some extent ☐

   c. Not at all ☐

6. How far do you think the Government at the Centre has been able to generate employment?

   a. To a large extent ☐ b. To some extent ☐

   c. Not at all ☐

7. How far do you think the Government at the Centre has been able to achieve a perceptible growth in different sectors?

Sector	*Extent of Satisfaction*		
	To a large extent	*To some extent*	*Not at all*
i. Agriculture			
ii. Industry			
iii. Health			
iv. Education			
v. Social			
vi. Any Other			

8. How far do you feel that the development has not been uniform in different decades after independence?

a. Generally not uniform ☐ b. Somewhat not uniform

c. Not at all uniform ☐

9. How far do you think that different regions have different levels of development?

a. To a large extent ☐ b. To some extent

c. Not at all ☐

10. How far do you think the country has witnessed unbalanced development?

a. To a large extent ☐ b. To some extent

c. Not at all ☐

C. PLAN PERSPECTIVE

1. In your opinion, how many Five-Year Plans have so far been launched? ____________________

2. Have you ever been associated with the planning process at any level during your service tenure?

Yes ☐ No ☐

3. If yes, please give the details of the same?

i. Level a. Village ☐ b. Block ☐ c. District ☐

d. State ☐

ii. Duration: Month / Years

4. How far do you think the planning process is:

Option	*Extent of Satisfaction*		
	To a large extent	*To some extent*	*Not at all*
i. Effective			
ii. Participative			
iii. Realistic			
iv. Efficient			

5. Which level of the planning process in your opinion is more?

Option	*Extent of Satisfaction*		
	To a large extent	*To some extent*	*Not at all*
i. Effective			
ii. Participative			
iii. Realistic			
iv. Efficient			

6. How far do you think the Five-Year Plans have served the purpose they were supposed to?

   a. To a large extent ☐ b. To some extent ☐

   c. Not at all ☐

7. Amongst the five decades of planned development, which of the following decade you consider as most fruitful and least fruitful?

	1950s	1960s	1970s	1980s	1990s
Most Fruitful					
Least Fruitful					

8. How far do you consider planning is an important strategy for development?

   a. To a large extent ☐ b. To some extent ☐

   c. Not at all ☐

9. How far do you feel satisfied with the planning system of India??

   a. To a large extent ☐ b. To some extent ☐

   c. Not at all ☐

10. What suggestions you have for improving the planning system at different levels in the country?

a. Central: __________
b. State: ____________
c. Local: ____________

D. PARADIGM OF DEVELOPMENT

1. How far do you think the Mahalnobis model helped Indian socio-economic development stabilize?

   a. To a large extent ☐ b. To some extent ☐

   c. Not at all ☐

2. How far do you think the mixed economy model suits India's requirements?

   a. To a large extent ☐ b. To some extent ☐

   c. Not at all ☐

3. How far do you think the capitalist model would suit India's development needs?

   a. To a large extent ☐ b. To some extent ☐

   c. Not at all ☐

4. How far do you think the socialistic model would meet India's development requirements?

   a. To a large extent ☐ b. To some extent ☐

   c. Not at all ☐

5. How far do you think the Dependency Syndrome has affected India's development?

   a. To a large extent ☐ b. To some extent ☐

   c. Not at all ☐

6. How far do you agree to have a state-sponsored development approach for the welfare of the people at large?

   a. To a large extent ☐ b. To some extent ☐

   c. Not at all ☐

7. How far do you willing to leave development at the pay of market forces?

   a. To a large extent ☐ b. To some extent ☐

   c. Not at all ☐

8. How far do you think to have a combination of the State and the Market for socio-economic growth?

   a. To a large extent ☐ b. To some extent ☐

   c. Not at all ☐

E. PARADIGM SHIFT

1. Are you aware of the paradigm shift in India's development focus?

   a. Yes ☐ b. No ☐

2. Do you see any policy change in the development process during the post-90s period?

   a. Yes ☐ b. No ☐

3. How far do you agree that the post-90s development of liberalisation and globalisation has helped Indian socio-economic development?

   a. To a large extent ☐ b. To some extent ☐

   c. Not at all ☐

4. How far do you think that the paradigm shift has helped the corporate sector?

   a. To a large extent ☐ b. To some extent ☐

   c. Not at all ☐

5. How far do you think the paradigm shift has helped the agriculture sector?

   a. To a large extent ☐ b. To some extent ☐

   c. Not at all ☐

6. How far do you think that the paradigm shift has helped the industrial sector?

   a. To a large extent ☐ b. To some extent ☐

   c. Not at all ☐

7. How far do you think that the paradigm shift has helped the urban middle class?

   a. To a large extent ☐ b. To some extent ☐

   c. Not at all ☐

8. How far do you think that the paradigm shift has helped the farmers at large?

   a. To a large extent ☐ b. To some extent ☐

   c. Not at all ☐

9. How far do you think the paradigm shift is a positive development?

   a. To a large extent ☐ b. To some extent ☐

   c. Not at all ☐

10. How far do you think the paradigm shift has ensured the development of less privileged sections?

    a. To a large extent ☐ b. To some extent ☐

    c. Not at all ☐

11. How far do you feel that the State should control the economy in the current scenario?

    a. To a large extent ☐ b. To some extent ☐

    c. Not at all ☐

12. How far are you satisfied with the role of the State in the changed scenario?

    a. To a large extent ☐ b. To some extent ☐

    c. Not at all ☐

Thank you

Signature of the Investigator: ______________________________

Name of the Investigator: ______________________________

Place: ______________________________

Date: ______________________________

A STUDY OF PARADIGM SHIFT IN INDIA'S DEVELOPMENT

QUESTIONNAIRE FOR NON-OFFICIALS

i. State:________________ ii. District:________________

iii. Block:________________ iv. Village:________________

A. GENERAL BACKGROUND

1. Name: ________________ 2. Age:________________
3. Sex: Male/Female________________
4. Political Position (if any):________________
5. Since when on the Position: ________________
6. Educational Qualification: ________________
7. Caste: ________________
8. Family Size – a. Adult: _______ b. Child: ______
9. Occupation: ________________
10. Monthly Income – a. Family: _________ b. Individual: ______

B. DEVELOPMENT PERSPECTIVE

1. How far do you feel satisfied with the development so far achieved in the country?

   a. To a large extent ☐ b. To some extent ☐

   c. Not at all ☐
2. How far do you feel satisfied with the role played by the State in development?

a. To a large extent ☐ b. To some extent ☐

c. Not at all ☐

3. How far are you satisfied with the role played by the Central Government in development?

   a. To a large extent ☐ b. To some extent ☐

   c. Not at all ☐

4. How far do you think your area has benefited from development effort of the government of India?

   a. To a large extent ☐ b. To some extent ☐

   c. Not at all ☐

5. How far do you feel satisfied with the role of your State Govt. in development?

   a. To a large extent ☐ b. To some extent ☐

   c. Not at all ☐

6. How far do you feel your State and the District has developed?

   A. Sate: a. To a large extent ☐ b. To some extent ☐

   c. Not at all ☐

   A. District: a. To a large extent ☐ b. To some extent ☐

   c. Not at all ☐

7. Do you consider your State as:

   a. Developed ☐ b. Developing ☐

   c. Under Developed ☐

8. Do you consider your District as:

   a. Developed ☐ b. Developing ☐

   c. Under Developed ☐

9. How far do think development has taken place in the district in the following sectors?

Sector	*Extent of Satisfaction*		
	To a large extent	*To some extent*	*Not at all*
i. Agriculture ii. Industry iii. Health iv. Education v. Social vi. Any Other			

10. How far do you think the development in your State / District has been balanced?

    A. Sate: a. To a large extent ☐ b. To some extent ☐

    c. Not at all ☐

    A. District: a. To a large extent ☐ b. To some extent ☐

    c. Not at all ☐

C. PLAN PERSPECTIVE

1. How far do you feel the Five-Year Plans have been able to achieve the desired goals?

   a. To a large extent ☐ b. To some extent ☐

   c. Not at all ☐

2. How far do you feel Five-Year Plans have been able to achieve the following in the country?

Activity	*Extent of Satisfaction*		
	To a large extent	*To some extent*	*Not at all*
i. Eradicate Poverty ii. Generate Employment iii. Improve Educational Services iv. Improve Health Services v. Achieve Total Literacy vi. Improve Agriculture vii. Develop Small Scale Industry viii. Animal Husbandry ix. Any other			

3. How far do you feel the Five-Year Plans have been able to achieve the following in the context of your state?

Activity	*Extent of Satisfaction*		
	To a large extent	*To some extent*	*Not at all*
i. Eradicate Poverty			
ii. Generate Employment			
iii. Improve Educational Services			
iv. Improve Health Services			
v. Achieve Total Literacy			
vi. Improve Agriculture			
vii. Develop Small Scale Industry			
viii. Animal Husbandry			
ix. Any other			

4. How far do you feel the Five-Year Plans have been able to achieve the following in the context of your district?

Activity	*Extent of Satisfaction*		
	To a large extent	*To some extent*	*Not at all*
i. Eradicate Poverty			
ii. Generate Employment			
iii. Improve Educational Services			
iv. Improve Health Services			
v. Achieve Total Literacy			
vi. Improve Agriculture			
vii. Develop Small Scale Industry			
viii. Animal Husbandry			
ix. Any other			

5. How far do you think the Five-Year Plans have been realistic?

   a. To a large extent ☐ b. To some extent ☐

   c. Not at all ☐

6. How far do you think the Five-Year Plans have served the interest of the weaker sections?

a. To a large extent ☐ b. To some extent ☐

c. Not at all ☐

7. How far do you think the strategies adopted by different Five-Year Plans have served the interest of the needy?

   a. To a large extent ☐ b. To some extent ☐

   c. Not at all ☐

8. How far do you think the Five-Year Plans have been able to instill change in the socio-economic sector?

   a. To a large extent ☐ b. To some extent ☐

   c. Not at all ☐

9. How far do you think the decentralised planning can help achieve better results?

   a. To a large extent ☐ b. To some extent ☐

   c. Not at all ☐

10. How far do you think decentralised planning has been affectively used in the country?

    a. To a large extent ☐ b. To some extent ☐

    c. Not at all ☐

D. PARADIGM OF DEVELOPMENT

1. How far do think the initial paradigm helped India stabilize?

   a. To a large extent ☐ b. To some extent ☐

   c. Not at all ☐

2. How far do you feel the big public sector investment helped Indian economy to stabilize?

   a. To a large extent ☐ b. To some extent ☐

   c. Not at all ☐

3. How far do think the earlier paradigm helped in the following

	Paradigm	*Extent of Satisfaction*		
		To a large extent	*To some extent*	*Not at all*
i.	Removing Income Disparity			
ii.	Increasing Employment in the Organised Sector			
iii.	Increasing Employment in Unorganised Sector			
iv.	Increasing Economic Growth			
v.	Eradicating Poverty			

4. How far do you feel the earlier paradigms have encouraged balanced regional growth?

   a. To a large extent ☐ b. To some extent ☐

   c. Not at all ☐

5. How far do you feel the earlier paradigms have encouraged unbalanced regional growth?

   a. To a large extent ☐ b. To some extent ☐

   c. Not at all ☐

6. How far do you feel satisfied with the paradigms followed so far?

   a. To a large extent ☐ b. To some extent ☐

   c. Not at all ☐

7. How far do you feel there is a need for change in the paradigm?

   a. To a large extent ☐ b. To some extent ☐

   c. Not at all ☐

E. PARADIGM SHIFT

1. How far do you feel the new paradigm has helped economic growth?

a. To a large extent ☐ b. To some extent ☐

c. Not at all ☐

2. How far do you feel the role of the State in development has been reduced?

a. To a large extent ☐ b. To some extent ☐

c. Not at all ☐

3. How far do you feel the new paradigm has helped the following:

	Item	*Extent of Satisfaction*		
		To a large extent	*To some extent*	*Not at all*
i.	Economic Growth			
ii.	Reducing Income Disparity			
iii.	Generating Employment			
iv.	Eradicating Poverty			
v.	Social Development			
vi.	Development of Infrastructure			

4. How far do think the new paradigm will help the disadvantaged sections of society?

a. To a large extent ☐ b. To some extent ☐

c. Not at all ☐

5. How far do think the new paradigm will help out the market force?

a. To a large extent ☐ b. To some extent ☐

c. Not at all ☐

6. How far do think the new paradigm will increase economic disparity?

a. To a large extent ☐ b. To some extent ☐

c. Not at all ☐

7. How far do think the new paradigm will serve societal cause?

   a. To a large extent ☐ b. To some extent ☐

   c. Not at all ☐

8. How far do think the new paradigm will serve the interest of the corporate sector?

   a. To a large extent ☐ b. To some extent ☐

   c. Not at all ☐

9. How far do you agree the new paradigm is market oriented?

   a. To a large extent ☐ b. To some extent ☐

   c. Not at all ☐

10. How far do you feel to change the existing paradigm?

    a. To a large extent ☐ b. To some extent ☐

    c. Not at all ☐

THE TABLES

OFFICIALS

B- DEVELOPMENT PERSPECTIVE

TABLE - 1

Q.1	How far do you think India has developed during the last five decades?		
	To a large extent	To some extent	Not at all
No.	8	1	0
%	88.89	11.11	0:00

TABLE - 2

Q.2	How far do you think the State should have a role in development?		
	To a large extent	To some extent	Not at all
No.	7	2	0
%	77.78	22.22	0.00

TABLE - 3

Q.3	How far are you satisfied with the role in India's development?		
	To a large extent	To some extent	Not at all
No.	5	4	0
%	55.56	44.44	0.00

TABLE - 4

Q.4	How far do you think the Government of the country has helped achieve development?		
	To a large extent	To some extent	Not at all
No.	4	5	0
%	44.44	55.56	0.00

TABLE - 5

Q.5	How far do you think the Government at the Centre been able to eradicate poverty?		
	To a large extent	To some extent	Not at all
No.	3	5	1
%	33.33	55.56	11.11

TABLE - 6

Q.6	**How far do you think the Government at the Centre has been able to generate employment?**		
	To a large extent	**To some extent**	**Not at all**
No.	4	2	3
%	44.44	22.22	33.33

TABLE - 7

Q.7		**How far do you think the Government at the Centre has been able to achieve a perceptible growth in different sectors?**		
		Extent of Satisfaction		
Sector		**To a large extent**	**To some extent**	**Not at all**
Agriculture	No.	9	0	0
	%	100.00	0.00	0.00
Industry	No.	2	7	0
	%	22.22	77.78	0.00
Health	No.	3	5	1
	%	33.33	55.56	11.11
Education	No.	4	5	0
	%	44.44	55.56	0.00
Social	No.	3	4	2
	%	33.33	44.44	22.22

TABLE - 8

Q.8	How far do you feel that the development has not been uniform in different decades after independence?		
	Generally not uniform	Somewhat not uniform	Not at all uniform
No.	4	4	1
%	44.44	44.44	11.11

TABLE - 9

Q.9	How far do you think that different regions have different levels of development?		
	To a large extent	To some extent	Not at all
No.	7	2	0
%	77.78	22.22	0.00

TABLE - 10

Q.10	How far do you the country has witnessed unbalanced development?		
	To a large extent	To some extent	Not at all
No.	5	4	0
%	55.56	44.44	0.00

C- PLAN PERSPECTIVE

TABLE - 11

Q.1	Have you ever been associated with the planning process ay any level during your service tenure?	
	Yes	No
No.	6	3
%	66.67	33.33

TABLE - 12

Q.2		**How far do you think the planning process is:**		
		Extent of Satisfaction		
Option		**To a large extent**	**To some extent**	**Not at all**
Effective	No.	2	7	0
	%	22.22	77.78	0.00
Participative	No.	3	6	0
	%	33.33	66.67	0.00
Realistic	No.	5	4	0
	%	55.56	44.44	0.00
Efficient	No.	4	4	1
	%	44.44	44.44	11.11

TABLE - 13

Q.3		**Which level of the planning process in your opinion is more?**			
		Extent of Satisfaction			
Option		**To a large extent**	**To some extent**	**Not at all**	**No response**
Effective	No.	2	1	2	4
	%	22.22	11.11	22.22	44.44
Participative	No.	3	1	2	3
	%	33.33	11.11	22.22	33.33
Realistic	No.	3	3	1	2
	%	33.33	33.33	11.11	22.22
Efficient	No.	2	1	2	4
	%	22.22	11.11	22.22	44.44

TABLE - 14

Q.4	How far do you think the Five-Year Plans have served the purpose they were supposed to?		
	To a large extent	To some extent	Not at all
No.	1	7	1
%	11.11	77.78	11.11

TABLE - 15

Q.5		Amongst the five decades of planned development, which of the following decade you consider as most fruitful and least fruitful.					
		1950s	1960s	1970s	1980s	1990s	No Response
Most Fruitful	No.	0	0	2	3	3	1
	%	0.00	0.00	22.22	33.33	33.33	11.11
Least Fruitful	No.	2	1	1	2	1	2
	%	22.22	11.11	11.11	22.22	11.11	22.22

TABLE - 16

Q.6	How far do you consider planning is an important strategy for development?		
	To a large extent	To some extent	Not at all
No.	6	3	0
%	66.67	33.33	0.00

TABLE - 17

Q.7	How far do you feel satisfied with the planning system of India?		
	To a large extent	To some extent	Not at all
No.	0	8	1
%	0.00	88.89	11.11

D- PARADIGM OF DEVELOPMENT

TABLE - 18

Q.1	How far do you think the Mahalnobis model helped Indian socio-economic development stabilize?		
	To a large extent	To some extent	Not at all
No.	2	6	1
%	22.22	66.67	11.11

TABLE - 19

Q.2	How far do you think the mixed economy model suits India's recruitments?		
	To a large extent	To some extent	Not at all
No.	3	4	2
%	33.33	44.44	22.22

TABLE - 20

Q.3	How far do you think the capitalist model would suit India's development needs?		
	To a large extent	To some extent	Not at all
No.	1	3	5
%	11.11	33.33	55.56

TABLE - 21

Q.4	How far do you think the socialistic model would meet India's development requirements?		
	To a large extent	To some extent	Not at all
No.	4	5	0
%	44.44	55.56	0.00

TABLE - 22

Q.5	How far do you think the Dependency Syndrome has affected India's development?		
	To a large extent	**To some extent**	**Not at all**
No. %	5 55.56	3 33.33	1 11.11

TABLE - 23

Q.6	How far do you agree to have a State-sponsored development approach for the welfare of the people at large?		
	To a large extent	**To some extent**	**Not at all**
No. %	4 44.44	5 55.56	0 0.00

TABLE - 24

Q.7	How far do you willing to leave development at the play of market forces?			
	To a large extent	**To some extent**	**Not at all**	**No response**
No. %	3 33.33	3 33.33	2 22.22	1 11.11

TABLE - 25

Q.8	How far do you think to have a combination of the State at the Market for socio-economic growth?			
	To a large extent	**To some extent**	**Not at all**	**No response**
No. %	3 33.33	3 33.33	1 11.11	2 22.22

E- PARADIGM SHIFT

TABLE - 26

Q.1	**Are you aware of the paradigm shift in India's development focus?**	
	Yes	**No**
No.	7	2
%	77.78	22.22

TABLE - 27

Q.2	**Do you see any policy change in the development process during the post-90s period?**	
	Yes	**No**
No.	6	33
%	66.67	33.33

TABLE - 28

Q.3	**How far do you agree that the post-90s development of liberalisation and globalisation has helped Indian socio-economic development?**		
	To a large extent	**To some extent**	**Not at all**
No.	3	3	3
%	33.33	33.33	33.33

TABLE - 29

Q.4	**How far do think that the paradigm shift has helped corporate sector?**		
	To a large extent	**To some extent**	**Not at all**
No.	4	4	1
%	44.44	44.44	11.11

TABLE - 30

Q.5	How far do think that the paradigm shift has helped agriculture sector?		
	To a large extent	**To some extent**	**Not at all**
No.	4	4	1
%	44.44	44.44	11.11

TABLE - 31

Q.6	How far do think that the paradigm shift has helped industrial sector?		
	To a large extent	**To some extent**	**Not at all**
No.	1	7	1
%	11.11	77.78	11.11

TABLE - 32

Q.7	How far do think that the paradigm shift has helped urban middle class?		
	To a large extent	**To some extent**	**Not at all**
No.	2	5	2
%	22.22	55.56	22.22

TABLE - 33

Q.8	How far do think that the paradigm shift has helped farmers at large?		
	To a large extent	**To some extent**	**Not at all**
No.	3	3	3
%	33.33	33.33	33.33

TABLE - 34

Q.9	How far do think that the paradigm shift is a positive development?		
	To a large extent	To some extent	Not at all
No. %	3 33.33	5 55.56	1 11.11

TABLE - 35

Q.10	How far do think that the paradigm shift has ensured the development of less privileged sections?		
	To a large extent	To some extent	Not at all
No. %	3 33.33	3 33.33	3 33.33

TABLE - 36

Q.11	How far do you feel that the State should control the economy in the current scenario?			
	To a large extent	To some extent	Not at all	No response
No.	4	4	0	1
%	44.44	44.44	0.00	11.11

TABLE - 37

Q.12	How far are you satisfied with the role of the State in the changed scenario?			
	To a large extent	To some extent	Not at all	No response
No.	1	6	1	1
%	11.11	66.67	11.11	11.11

NON- OFFICIALS

B- DEVELOPMENT PERSPECTIVE

TABLE - 1

Q.1	How far do you feel satisfied with the development so far achieved in the country?		
	To a large extent	To some extent	Not at all
No. %	2 13.33	9 60.00	4 26.67

TABLE - 2

Q.2	How far do you feel satisfied with the role played by the State in development?		
	To a large extent	To some extent	Not at all
No.	2	7	6
%	13.33	46.67	40.00

TABLE - 3

Q.3	How far do you feel satisfied with the role played by the Central Government in development?		
	To a large extent	To some extent	Not at all
No. %	2 13.33	6 40.00	4 26.67

TABLE - 4

Q.4	How far do you think your area has benefited from development effort of the Government of India?		
	To a large extent	To some extent	Not at all
No. %	3 20.00	5 33.33	7 46.67

TABLE - 5

Q.5	**How far do you feel satisfied with the role of your State Govt. in development?**		
	To a large extent	**To some extent**	**Not at all**
No.	1	8	6
%	6.67	53.33	40.00

TABLE - 6

Q.6	**How far do you feel your State and the District has developed?**			
		To a large extent	**To some extent**	**Not at all**
A. State	**No.**	1	7	7
	%	6.67	46.67	46.67
B. District	**No.**	3	5	7
	%	20.00	33.33	46.67

TABLE - 7

Q.7	**Do you consider your State as:**		
	Developed	**Developing**	**Under Developed**
No.	0	9	6
%	0.00	60.00	40.00

TABLE - 8

Q.8	**Do you consider your District as:**		
	Developed	**Developing**	**Under Developed**
No.	2	8	5
%	13.33	53.33	33.33

TABLE - 9

Q.9		How far do think development has taken place in the District in the following sectors–		
		Extent of Satisfaction		
Sector		**To a large extent**	**To some extent**	**Not at all**
Agriculture	No.	8	5	2
	%	53.33	33.33	13.33
Industry	No.	1	5	9
	%	6.67	33.33	60.00
Health	No.	4	6	5
	%	26.67	40.00	33.33
Education	No.	6	6	3
	%	40.00	40.00	20.00
Social	No.	2	7	6
	%	13.33	46.67	40.00

TABLE - 10

Q.10		How far do you think the development in your State / District has been balanced?		
		To a large extent	**To some extent**	**Not at all**
A. State	No.	2	6	7
	%	13.33	40.00	46.67
B. District	No.	3	7	5
	%	20.00	46.67	33.33

C- PLAN PERSPECTIVE

TABLE - 11

Q.1	How far do you feel the Five-Year Plans have been able to achieve the desired goals?		
	To a large extent	**To some extent**	**Not at all**
No.	0	8	7
%	0.00	53.33	46.67

TABLE - 12

Q.2		How far do think development has taken place in the District in the following sectors		
		Extent of Satisfaction		
Activity		To a large extent	To some extent	Not at all
i. Eradicate Poverty	No.	1	4	10
	%	6.67	26.67	66.67
ii. Generate Employment	No.	0	6	9
	%	0.00	40.00	60.00
iii. Improve Educational	No.	2	10	3
Services	%	13.33	66.67	20.00
iv. Improve Health	No.	1	8	6
Services	%	6.67	53.33	40.00
v. Achieve Total	No.	1	9	5
literacy	%	6.67	60.00	33.33
vi. Improve	No.	4	9	2
Agriculture	%	26.67	60.00	13.33
vii. Develop Small	No	3	3	9
Scale Industry	%	20.00	20.00	60.00
viii. Animal	No.	1	10	4
Husbandry	%	6.67	66.67	26.67

TABLE - 13

Q.3		How far do you feel the Five Year Plans have been able to achieve the following in the context of your state?		
		Extent of Satisfaction		
Activity		To a large extent	To some extent	Not at all
ix. Eradicate	No.	1	5	9
Poverty	%	6.67	33.33	60.00
x. Generate	No.	0	5	10
Employment	%	0.00	33.33	66.67
xi Improve Educa-	No.	2	7	6
tional Services	%	13.33	46.67	40.00

xii. Improve Health Services	No. %	1 6.67	6 40.00	8 53.33
xiii. Achieve Total Literacy	No. %	1 6.67	8 53.33	6 40.00
xiv. Improve Agriculture	No. %	6 40.00	7 46.67	2 13.33
xv. Develop Small Scale Industry	No. %	1 6.67	8 53.33	6 40.00
xvi. Animal Husbandry	No. %	1 6.67	10 66.67	4 26.67

TABLE - 14

Q.4		How far do you feel the Five Year Plans have been able to achieve the following in the context of your district?		
		Extent of Satisfaction		
Activity		To a large extent	To some extent	Not at all
i. Eradicate Poverty	No. %	2 13.33	5 33.33	8 53.33
ii. Generate Employment	No. %	2 13.33	4 26.67	9 60.00
iii. Improve Educational Services	No. %	4 26.67	6 40.00	5 33.33
iv. Improve Health Services	No. %	3 20.00	5 33.33	7 46.67
v. Achieve Total literacy	No. %	2 13.33	8 53.33	5 33.33
vi. Improve Agriculture	No. %	7 46.67	4 26.67	4 26.67
vii. Develop Small Scale Industry	No. %	4 26.67	5 33.33	6 40.00
viii. Animal Husbandry	No. %	2 13.33	11 73.33	2 13.33

TABLE - 15

Q.5	How far do you think the Five-Year Plans have been realistic?		
	To a large extent	To some extent	Not at all
No.	3	6	6
%	20.00	40.00	40.00

TABLE - 16

Q.6	How far do you think the Five-Year Plans have served the interest of the weaker sections?		
	To a large extent	To some extent	Not at all
No.	7	6	2
%	46.67	40.00	13.33

TABLE - 17

Q.7	How far do you think the strategies adopted by different Five-Year Plans have served the interest of the needy?		
	To a large extent	To some extent	Not at all
No.	5	5	5
%	33.33	33.33	33.33

TABLE - 18

Q.8	How far do you think the Five-Year Plans have been able to instill change in the socio-economic sector?		
	To a large extent	To some extent	Not at all
No.	2	7	6
%	13.33	46.67	40.00

TABLE - 19

Q.9	How far do you think the decentralised planning can help achieve better results?		
	To a large extent	**To some extent**	**Not at all**
No.	4	3	8
%	26.67	20.00	53.33

TABLE - 20

Q.10	How far do you think decentralised planning has been affectively used in the country?		
	To a large extent	**To some extent**	**Not at all**
No.	3	6	6
%	20.00	40.00	40.00

D- PARADIGM OF DEVELOPMENT

TABLE - 21

Q.1	How far do think the initial paradigm helped India stabilize?		
	To a large extent	**To some extent**	**Not at all**
No.	0	10	5
%	0.00	66.67	33.33

TABLE - 22

Q.2	How far do you feel the big public sector investment helped Indian economy to stabilize?		
	To a large extent	**To some extent**	**Not at all**
No.	1	8	6
%	6.67	53.33	40.00

TABLE - 23

Q.3		**How far do you feel the big public sector investment helped Indian economy to stabilize?**			
		Extent of Help			
Paradigm		**To a large extent**	**To some extent**	**Not at all**	**No Response**
i. Removing Income Disparity	No. %	0 0.00	5 33.33	10 66.67	0 0.00
ii. Increasing Employment in the organised sector	No. %	0 0.00	4 26.67	11 73.33	0 0.00
iii. Increasing Employment in unorganised sector	No. %	0 0.00	5 33.33	10 66.67	0 0.00
iv. Increasing Economic Growth	No. %	1 6.67	6 40.00	8 53.33	0 0.00
v. Eradicating Poverty	No. %	1 6.67	3 20.00	10 66.67	1 6.67

TABLE - 24

Q.4	**How far do you feel the earlier paradigms have encouraged balanced regional growth?**		
	To a large extent	**To some extent**	**Not at all**
No.	1	6	8
%	6.67	40.00	53.33

TABLE - 25

Q.5	How far do you feel the earlier paradigms have encouraged unbalanced regional growth?		
	To a large extent	**To some extent**	**Not at all**
No.	3	7	5
%	20.00	46.67	33.33

TABLE - 26

Q.6	How far do you feel satisfied with the paradigms followed so far?		
	To a large extent	**To some extent**	**Not at all**
No.	3	4	8
%	20.00	26.67	53.33

TABLE - 27

Q.7	How far do you feel there is a need for change in the paradigm?			
	To a large extent	**To some extent**	**Not at all**	**No Response**
No.	7	5	2	1
%	46.67	33.33	13.33	6.67

E- PARADIGM SHIFT

TABLE - 28

Q.1	How far do you feel the new paradigm has helped economic growth?		
	To a large extent	**To some extent**	**Not at all**
No.	2	6	7
%	13.33	40.00	46.67

TABLE - 29

Q.2	How far do you feel the role of the State in development has been reduced?		
	To a large extent	To some extent	Not at all
No.	1	4	10
%	6.67	26.67	66.67

TABLE - 30

Q.3 How far do you feel the new paradigm has helped the following:					
			Extent of Help		
Item			To a large extent	To some extent	Not at all
i.	Economic Growth	No. %	2 13.33	3 20.00	10 66.67
ii.	Reducing Income Disparity	No. %	3 20.00	3 20.00	9 60.00
iii.	Generating Employment	No. %	3 20.00	1 6.67	11 73.33
iv.	Eradicating Poverty	No. %	3 20.00	1 6.67	11 73.33
v.	Social Development	No. %	2 13.33	5 33.33	8 53.33
vi.	Development of Infrastructure	No. %	2 13.33	7 46.67	6 40.00

TABLE - 31

Q.4	How far do think the new paradigm will help the disadvantaged sections of society?		
	To a large extent	To some extent	Not at all
No.	5	1	9
%	33.33	6.67	60.00

TABLE -32

Q.5	How far do think the new paradigm will help out the market force?		
	To a large extent	**To some extent**	**Not at all**
No.	3	4	8
%	20.00	26.67	53.33

TABLE - 33

Q.6	How far do think the new paradigm will increase economic disparity?		
	To a large extent	**To some extent**	**Not at all**
No.	4	5	6
%	26.67	33.33	40.00

TABLE - 34

Q.7	How far do think the new paradigm will serve societal cause?		
	To a large extent	**To some extent**	**Not at all**
No.	2	6	7
%	13.33	40.00	46.67

TABLE - 35

Q.8	How far do think the new paradigm will serve the interest of the corporate sector?		
	To a large extent	**To some extent**	**Not at all**
No.	6 6	2	1
%	40.00 40.00	13.33	6.67

TABLE - 36

Q.9	How far do you agree the new paradigm is market oriented?		
	To a large extent	**To some extent**	**Not at all**
No.	5	8	2
%	33.33	53.33	13.33

TABLE - 37

Q.10	How far do you feel to change the existing paradigm?		
	To a large extent	**To some extent**	**Not at all**
No.	10	4	1
%	66.67	26.67	6.67

Bibliography

The Concept of Development: An Issue in the Study of Human Behaviour, (Ed.) Dale B. Harris, University of Minnesota Press, Minnopolis, 1957.

Culture and Development: Cultural Pattern in Areas of Under Development, Alexander K.C. and Kumaran, K.P., Sage Publication, New Delhi, 1962.

Society, Culture and Development, Mukharjee, Ram Krishna, Sage Publication, New Delhi, 1991.

The Development Debate, S.P. Srivastava, Rawat Publication, Jaipur, 1998.

United Nation, Measures for the Economic Development of Under—Developed Countries (New York, 1951).

The Right to Development: A Primer, Centre for Development and Human Right, Sage Publication, New Delhi, 2004.

Five-Year Plans, Planning Commission, Government of India, New Delhi (From First to Tenth Five-Year Plan).

Sustainable Rural Development, Andrew Shephord, Palgrave, New York, 2001.

Poverty Curtain: Choices For the Third World, Mahbub-ul-Haq, 1985.

Human Development Report, UNDP, 2005.

U.P. Development Report, Planning Commission, Government of India, New Delhi, 2007.

Land and People, (U.P.) and (Karnataka), (Ed.) S.C. Bhatt and Gopal K. Bhargava, Kalpaz Publication, Delhi, 2005.

Index

R

S

T

U

V

W